INTIMATE
RELATIONSHIPS

BY THE SAME AUTHOR

Trances People live:
Healing Approaches in Quantum Psychology.

Quantum Consciousness:
The Guide to Experiencing Quantum Psychology.

The Dark Side of the Inner Child:
The Next Step.

The Tao of Chaos:
Quantum Consciousness, Volume II.

Hearts on Fire:
The Tao of Meditation and
the Roots of Quantum Psychology.

The Way of the Human, Vol. I:
Developing Multi-Dimensional Awareness

The Way of the Human, Vol. II:
The False Core-False Self.

The Way of the Human, Vol. III:
Beyond Quantum Psychology.

Beginner's Guide to Quantum Psychology

I AM THAT I AM:
A Tribute to Sri Nisargadatta Maharaj

INTIMATE RELATIONSHIPS

WHY THEY DO
AND DO NOT WORK

By
STEPHEN H. WOLINSKY, PH.D.

ALL OF THE PROBLEMS THAT MEN AND
WOMEN FACE IN THEIR RELATIONSHIPS
ARE THOUSANDS OF YEARS OLD,
THEY HAVE NEVER CHANGED. IT IS ONLY
OUR WAY OF THINKING AND TALKING ABOUT
THEM THAT HAS CHANGED.

Stephen H. Wolinsky

DEDICATION

To my divine Leni, my lifelong partner

To my parents for teaching me about boundaries

ACKNOWLEDGEMENTS

Allen Horne for his excellent editorial work

Susan Mathews-Scott
for her case examples

Dorothy & Frank Agneesens
for teaching Carol about love

Carol Agneesens
for her article on the Biology of Relationships

THE AUTHOR

Stephen H. Wolinsky, Ph.D., began his clinical practice in Los Angeles, California in 1974. A Gestalt and Reichian therapist and trainer, he led workshops in Southern California. He was also trained in Classical Hypnosis, Psychosynthesis, Psychodrama/Psychomotor, and Transactional Analysis. In 1977 he journeyed to India, where he lived for almost six years studying meditation. He moved to New Mexico in 1982 to resume a clinical practice. There he began to train therapists in Ericksonian Hypnosis and family therapy. Dr. Wolinsky also conducted year-long trainings entitled: "Integrating Hypnosis with Psychotherapy," and "Integrating Hypnosis with Family Therapy."

Dr. Wolinsky is the author of *Trances People Live: Healing Approaches in Quantum Psychology®*, *Quantum Consciousness: The Guide to Experiencing Quantum Psychology®*, *The Tao of Chaos: Quantum Consciousness Volume II*, *The Dark Side of the Inner Child*; and *Hearts on Fire: The Roots of Quantum Psychology*. He has recently completed a trilogy, *The Way of the Human: The Quantum Psychology Notebooks*. *The Beginner's Guide to Quantum Psychology* and *I Am That I Am: A Tribute to Sri Nisargadatta Maharaj*. He is the founder of Quantum Psychology® and lives in Capitola, California. He can be reached for workshop information at (831) 464-0564 or by FAX at (831) 479-8233.

TABLE OF CONTENTS

INTRODUCTION

THE RELATIONSHIP PUZZLE

Why write a book on the reasons relationships do not work? At the present time, all you see in the marketplace is why they should work, could work, ought to work, and how to make them work. When I thought about why relationships do not work, as usual, I decided to look at myself and my clients, friends and workshop participants. The question I pondered was, Why hadn't my relationships in the past worked? Was it something that I had done wrong? Was it something that I should have done? Was there something wrong with me? Or was it that there was something wrong with the situation. After all we had met each other on so many levels—*what happened*? In my travels around the world, I have met lots of people, and it is clear that most everyone wants to have an intimate relationship. And yet often, they can't seem to get it together. Why not?

In 1996, when I was in the middle of writing *The Way of The Human Trilogy* and as I began to examine the relationships in my life over the last forty-something years, a pattern emerged. There was something I either wasn't aware of or didn't want to acknowledge. In *The Way of the Human*, I talked about the development of the False Core-False Self and the different dimensions of manifestation and awareness. Suddenly in a flash, I thought, Well, why not apply the concepts of *separation* and child development, and the different levels of awareness, to relationships. Maybe there is some correlation that can reveal the problems in *intimate relationships and why they do and don't work?*

In order to discover why relationships do work, we must first discover why they don't work.

I began to look at relationship problems in the light of developmental psychology, in general; and, specifically at the shock of the Realization of Separation, which was discussed in Volume II of the *The Way of the Human* trilogy. What is this shock trauma? It is the sudden Realization of Separation from mom that an infant has between the age of 5-12 months. This shock response gets resisted so intensely that, like dominoes falling, it affects all future relationships. This shock response, and its impact on intimate relationships, led me to understand why relationships do not work and lead to; 1) misperceptions and relationship distortions; 2) *unrealistic expectations* linked to the separation response; and 3) confusion of the dimensions of manifestation and awareness, caused by the shock response.

With this in mind, suddenly it hit me how obvious it was, and just as suddenly the relationship puzzle came together and I understood why intimate relationships do not work. In fact, it was so obvious that I could understand how it had gone unseen.

Before we get too far ahead of ourselves, we need to understand the shock trauma of the Realization of Separation. This trauma of separation, when left unresolved, leads to *expectations* of merger. These *expectations* of, and resistance to merger are *past time* wounds, and because of the wounds from the shock of the Realization of Separation, people lose their present-time humanness and go into a past-time trance. Soon, they confuse the levels of manifestation, and by substituting one level for another, hope to heal the shock wound and promote merging. These past time shocks of separation and resistance to separation lead to unsatisfactory outcomes and *expectations* of merger, which directly affect our *intimate relationships and why they do and do not work*.

This book focuses on relationship problems associated with separation. It is the symptoms of separation *often masked*, which arise in relationships, which we can use as a pointer or a signpost which can lead us to the root cause of relationship problems. In this way, I think it can offer useful explanations to the following problems and questions: 1) How and why you got where you are; 2) the problems you are facing; and 3) various remedies to deal with them. To begin with, first you have to determine where you are in a relationship and what is missing; next, why it does or does not work; and third, how to *stop deceiving yourself by going into a trance which denies what is happening*. In this way, the precious time of your life is not wasted on wishing and hoping.

Years ago I was having dinner with two women friends, and one of them was talking about relationships and all the different men she had met. "Well, men should be like rocks," the other women said, "you pick one up, look at it, and hold it for a minute. You see if you want to keep this particular rock. If the answer is yes, you do. But if the answer's no, put it down. Just don't carry it around uselessly."

THE RELATIONSHIP MAP

We all know that *the map isn't the territory* and that people aren't maps; but nevertheless, this book could be viewed as a map. It has signposts to help you determine where you are in your relationships, and what your relationship problems are based on. In short, where and at what levels the relationship works for you and where it does not. Hopefully, with this book, you can either move beyond the problems, or beyond the relationship. Which leaves us with the immortal words of Dionne Warwick: "Wishin' and hopin' and thinkin' and prayin', plannin' and dreamin'". . . , won't make it be different than the way it is.

Good luck,
    With love,
        Your brother Stephen

IT IS OUR DEEP RESISTANCE TO THE
SHOCK OF THE REALIZATION OF
SEPARATION WHICH ORGANIZES
OUR PERSONAL PAIN; AND
WHICH LATER LEADS US TO OUR
CHOICE OF A PARTNER AS A
FANTASIZED PERSONAL SAVIOR
WHO WILL LEAD US TO HEAVEN
(*RE-MERGER*).

Stephen H. Wolinsky

PROLOGUE

THE RELATIONSHIP PROBLEM MADE SIMPLE

After completing *The Way of the Human* trilogy, I began to apply its approach to relationships. My curiosity led me to ask, "What are the ingredients in a relationship which make it work or not." I also began to realize that we all live on different levels of manifestation and awareness, each level with its own intrinsic value, function and importance.

Wherein lies the problem then? The problem is that with separation, resistance to separation, and *expectations* of merger, we substitute and, consequently, confuse one level of manifestation for another as we attempt to resolve the pain of separation. To put a nice spin on it, it can be said that we are trying to resolve the problem of the shock of the Realization of Separation; but actually it is a self-perpetuating resistance to separation which keeps the pattern going.

To clarify, an infant who experiences separation and desires *re-merger* must look for ways to accomplish this, some of which work while others don't. For this reason, the behaviors and levels of manifestation which bring merger or resist separation are over-stressed and emphasized; and those which do not bring merger, or bring about separation, are resisted, attempted to be compensated for, or ignored.

RELATIONSHIP PROBLEMS AND COMPLAINTS

Because problems arise in relationships in order to resist past separation and strive for merger, we often relate at one level but not at another. We then mistakenly or unknowingly substitute, confuse or lose awareness of other levels. Certainly all of us can relate to the following issues and dilemmas: "Well, I could relate to him at an emotional level, but not at an intellectual level." "I can relate to him in the external world" [i.e., we like playing tennis or we work in the same business] but on an emotional level, he is unavailable." "Our sex life is great, but we just don't have anything to say to each other." "We feel a real heart resonance, and we enjoy doing things together and share a lot emotionally, but we're not sexually turned on to each other." "There's something missing in the relationship but I don't know what it is."

All of these familiar complaints might begin to shine a light of understanding into *intimate relationships*, and why they work and don't work.

ONE

WHY RELATIONSHIP?

At first glance, this may seem like a simple question. But on deeper investigation, we may discover unacknowledged motives for being with the specific person we are with, or for being in a relationship altogether. If we examine these reasons with honesty, we might be able to understand more about ourselves and our relationships.

On a biological, instinctual level, we human beings have the drive to mate and the urge to merge. The body craves human touch, contact and interaction, sexual intimacy, and companionship. These are basic, biological needs, and part of being human.

Beyond the biological level though, we all have varying needs which seek fulfillment and expression in relationships. These occur in the other dimensions of manifestation, and are based on our own personal values and individual personalities. We may want a companion to share our daily life's events with. We may want emotional support. We may long for a partner to discuss ideas with or perhaps spirituality. We may seek a deep love and trust that grows with time through life's experiences. We may wish to feel special to someone, to know that we really matter to another. Perhaps the sense of belonging is a strong motivating factor. We may want to feel the security that someone is there for us in times of need.

All or any of these reasons may be present for us in the search for a mate. And the driver of all of these is genetics, the biological mating-merger response and the survival of the species.

THE TRIGGER

Huge ★ ★ ★ ★

When the past time shock of the Realization of Separation is experienced, pain can be triggered. What may be unacknowledged is that, in order to avoid painful feelings, beliefs, or a poor self-image, we might stay in a relationship which does not provide nourishment for us. There are individuals who barely take any time or space between relationships, in order to avoid painful feelings of separation. This deep resistance to separation is behind many people staying in unpleasant relationships. For example, if one has a deep fear of being unloved, then being in a relationship, however unhealthy, might provide a buffer against inner gnawing emptiness and anxiety.

People may seek a relationship in order to compensate for feelings of having no worth or love. For them, being in a relationship gives the illusion of having a necessary component or missing external piece which is *expected* to bring about an internal sense of well-being. And so, to avoid the pain of lovelessness, worthlessness, and separation, people will maintain a relationship even if it's at the expense of their own well being. In short; *they will avoid separation at all costs.*

EXERCISE:

Below is an exercise.

Take a few minutes to write down your answers and see what you come up with.

By answering these questions honestly, we can begin to see what we are avoiding or striving for in a relationship to overcome our own feelings.

Write down your answers and notice what, if anything, arises*:*

1. Have you ever stayed in a relationship as a way to not experience: The belief that something was inherently wrong with you? *NO*
   Write down your answers and notice what, if anything, arises.

2. Have you ever stayed in a relationship as a way to not experience: Feelings of worthlessness?
   Write down your answers and notice what, if anything, arises.

3. Have you ever stayed in a relationship as a way to not experience: The feeling that you can't do? *NO*
   Write down your answers and notice what, if anything, arises.

4. Have you ever stayed in a relationship as a way to not experience: Feelings of inadequacy? *Yes*
   Write down your answers and notice what, if anything, arises. *Yes — In the Past NOT NOW*

3

5. Have you ever stayed in a relationship as a way to not experience: The fear that you do not exist?
   Write down your answers and notice what, if anything, arises.   Yes— But Not Van

6. Have you ever stayed in a relationship as a way to not experience: The feeling of being alone?
   Write down your answers and notice what, if anything, arises.

7. Have you ever stayed in a relationship as a way to not experience: The feeling of being incomplete?
   Write down your answers and notice what, if anything, arises.

8. Have you ever stayed in a relationship as a way to not experience: The feeling of being powerless?
   Write down your answers and notice what, if anything, arises.

9. Have you ever stayed in a relationship as a way to not experience: The feeling of separation?
   Write down your answers and notice what, if anything, arises.

10. Have you ever stayed in a relationship as a way to not experience: The feeling you have no love or are unlovable?
    Write down your answers and notice what, if anything, arises.

11. Have you ever remained in an unhealthy or unfulfilling relationship in order to not experience: Any of the above?

CONCLUSION

Hopefully, these questions will help to get us to focus in on why we are in a relationship, and if we are avoiding something within ourselves.

TWO

THE FALSE CORE-
FALSE SELF EXPLAINED

AN OVERVIEW OF
THE FALSE CORE-FALSE SELF

Before we go further, we need to discuss the False Core-False Self and how it functions in our lives and in our relationships. If we really dig down to our deepest resisted feelings of separation and their associated beliefs, what emerges is called the False Core. It is the one concept, the one idea, the one belief structure, we hold about ourselves, which organizes our entire psychology and gives us a reason for the separation. Most often, we seek a relationship or specific type of individual with the expectation of overcoming and resisting the False Core, or which re-enforces the False Core, and the shock of the Realization of Separation. In addition, these dreaded feelings of separation which created the False Core in the first place may cause a desperate, flight-flight response when a relationship is perceived or (mis)perceived as being threatened.

The False Self is the strategy that we develop and use to overcome the False Core. It is the False Self which may choose to stay in a relationship so as not to feel separate, unloved, worthless or to compensate for a False Core of alone, power-less, etc. This strategy of the False Self to overcome the False Core perpetuates the problem because the False Core-False Self is actually a holographic unit, one cannot exist without the other, *but both are false*. Thus, though we try to over-come painful feelings, we wind up causing them to continue. Dysfunctional strategies are developed and implemented by the False Self to maintain a relationship, even at the cost of an individual's own well-being.

THE FALSE CORE

The False Core is that one conclusion that you have about yourself which holds your entire psychology together and organizes not only your every thought, emotion, action, fan-tasy, and reaction, etc., but also how you imagine others see you. In *Trances People Live* (1986), I call this the *Organiz-ing Principle.* The False Core organizes our view of the world, our view of ourselves, and how we imagine the world views us, along with an emotional component.

It is crucial to explore the False Core because if you be-lieve in a false premise, then all of the premises which follow the false premise must also be false. It's as if you were build-ing a house or a relationship on shifting sands, and were try-ing to compensate for its weak foundation by using bricks to make it stable. In this case, the bricks are either psychology or spirituality. Because it is not supported solidly in the ground, and does not have a solid or stable foundation, it will floun-der especially with the least change in your external context,

RELATIONSHIP PSYCHOLOGY PRINCIPLE

The False Core conclusion can only lead to more False conclusions and to more False solutions because the conclusions and solutions are not based in present time reality.

THE ORIGIN OF THE FALSE CORE

How does the False Core develop? To understand this process, we use the *lens* or *story* of Psychoanalytic Developmental Psychology, which theorizes that newborn children believe that they and their mother are one, and that between 5-12 months realize that they are separate from their mother. Relationship Psychology theorizes that the False Core is the false reason or false conclusion children draw to explain why they are separate. In this way, the False Core provides the infant with a *False Cause*. Once the False Cause is believed, the mind can then create a solution or False Self to overcome this False Cause. This trauma of separation is called the *narcissistic wound* or *narcissistic injury*. The solution to this False Core or Cause is based on a False conclusion, and hence, it too is also false. It is from this False conclusion, that a False Self emerges to hide, overcome, transform, heal, resist, deny, and in a word, overcompensate for the False Core. Once solidified, the False Core-False Self seals your psycho-emotional, your relationship, and even your spiritual fate.

When children experience themselves as separate from mom, the shock to the nervous system causes a narcissistic wound or injury. At the moment of this shock, an infant's False Core begins to solidify. This False Core is what they *conclude* about themselves and why and what their separation from Mom means. Thus, a *False Cause* is attributed to this natural separation process. Examples include, "I am separate *because* I'm worthless," "I am separate *because* I'm inadequate," "I am separate *because* I don't exist," "I am separate *because* I'm powerless," and many others. As a result of their False Core conclusion, people might unknowingly spend the rest of their lives re-living it in relationship in order prove that it is true (self-fulfilling prophecy) or, if they are compensated by the False Self, trying to overcome it or prove it is not true.

You then might form all of your future relationships as a way to deal with the trauma caused by the shock of the Realization of Separation, by trying to overcome it, heal it, resist it, hide it, resolve it, transform it, spiritualize it, or to re-enforce the False Core. But remember, the False Core is a concept, a False Cause which you believe is real; and any solution based on a False conclusion can only yield further False conclusions and solutions. For this reason, because the False Self is a concept which occurs *after* the False Core and the shock of the Realization of Separation, it is based on the earlier False conclusion and more false than the False Core itself.

An example might be that someone who feels "I am worthless" might search for a relationship, or be attracted to a partner who unknowingly plays out the other side of the False Core. For example, if your False Core is "I am worthless," you might unconsciously be attracted to someone who provides worth (False Self), or if you feel, unlovable (False Core), you might be attracted to a spiritual system as a relationship, or a relationship which believes some form of "love conquers all." In Relationship Psychology, the concept of "I am worthless" is defined as a False conclusion. Instead of trying to work it out or act it out in relation to another, you need to see it for what it is, a False conclusion and work it out with yourself by questioning it and ultimately discarding it.

The False Core Driver is the underlying conclusion, premise, concept, belief, or idea you hold about yourself which drives your psychology and all you think you are. By being brought to the light of consciousness and "on screen," we can learn to confront, question, enquire, dismantle, and go beyond it. As my teacher Nisargadatta Maharaj said, "In order to let go of something, you must first know what it is." The False Core Driver can be compared to the unconscious mind.

The False Core Driver runs on its own, like a machine on automatic. Therefore, it is imperative in order to have an intimate relationship to: 1) Stop the machinery; 2) enquire into its relevance; 3) dismantle it; and 4) go beyond it.

HOW TO DISCOVER YOUR FALSE CORE

To determine your False Core or False Core Driver, take notice of whatever it is you are experiencing and then trace it back by asking yourself, "What is the worst of that?" or "What is so bad about that?" When you trace it back, you'll eventually hit the bottom or one of the False Cores: In this way, you can see if you are again playing out your False Core-False Self in relationship.

DISMANTLING THE FALSE CORE

Your False Core and how it interacts in your relationship is essential.

If you study the False Core it demonstrates the organization of the personality which, in turn, leads us to understand who we think we are, and how we function in relationships. The purpose of discovering your False Core-False Self is to find out who you imagine you are—but are actually not and then discarding it. In this way, you can find out who you are first and avoid relationship problems at last.

The False Core is invisible to you because you think it *is* you. For example, "I *always* feel inadequate," "I *always* feel worthless" or "I *always* feel alone," are False Cores which are never questioned because they are so interwoven into the fabric of "you" and "your" life that you do not see them. They are transparent, like looking through a glass of which you are unaware. In the same way, you see the world and yourself through this pane (pain) of glass, this lens or frame, which you think is you, without realizing it is a lens.

As stated earlier, the False Core organizes your entire psychological frame. You only have one False Core, but you have an infinite number of ways of defending against it. Defending means trying to overcome it or resist it in some way.

THE FALSE SELF

> ### RELATIONSHIP PRINCIPLE
>
> Any person in a relationship whose unconscious aim is to transform or change the False Core of another is organized by their False Self and is driven by their False Core. Hence, it can only re-enforce the relationship pain cycle.

How you resist your False Core, try to overcome your False Core, heal your False Core, hide your False Core, spiritualize your False Core, transform your False Core, or justify your False Core, etc.—all of these are handled by your False Self which acts as a compensator. Furthermore, in relationships how you handle another's False Core is done by your False Self, in a projective attempt to handle your own False Core. For example, if your False Core is "I am inadequate," to compensate you might get very analytic. If your partner's False Core is Alone, when he gets into Alone, you might feel your own False Core. So instead of dealing with your False Core you put your attention on him, you get analytic with him. This is one way that a False Self can act toward another in relationship so as to avoid its False Core. Furthermore, the False Self acts as a buffer in the way we present ourselves to the world and our relationship partner, i.e., our socially acceptable masks, how we want to be seen, or see ourselves to avoid the shock of past-time separation projected on present-time.

In relationships we oftentimes in the beginning present the False Self adaptive identity image automatically. Unfortunately, we forget, and so does our prospective partner, that the identity is fake, something that was made up, not real, a creation. As the years go by, we wonder why we feel alienated and misunderstood in relationship, not realizing it is the result of being stuck in the False Core-False Self complex. More importantly, our "new" relationship partner feels confused too, why is she/he different from how they presented themselves (False Self).

The False Self mask is the presentation; and, unfortunately, in America and now in Western Europe, people spend lots of time working on their image and presentation, not realizing it is a False Self. In this way, at first we are attracted to a false presentation, which masks the False Core. In other words, *at first* people are more interested in the *"sizzle than they are in the steak."* Take, for example, a sexual relationship where we can't say what we need because it might be considered crude or uncool. Instead, we pretend. We create a fantasy and hide our true feelings in the vain hope that somehow we'll get what we want. This is the nature of the False Self—to defend against our impulses, feelings, and drives, and to buffer and hide the False Core. It forces us to *split off* from our somatic and animal selves, creating an image and hiding, our true feelings.

Recall a time when you felt angry or upset with your partner, and put up a false front to hide it from the world. Or a time when you felt sexually turned on with a prospective partner, and pretended you weren't by acting as if you were indifferent. These examples are the False Self in action.

We deny our feelings in favor of a False Self, which is actually an image, act, or presentation, which we fall in love with and try to get others to do the same. This is like the story of Narcissus who fell in love with his own image. But this is unsatisfying because we know it is False, and so any love we receive can never be "taken in." In this way, the False Self not only defends against the False Core but it denies our bodily sensations and animal nature.

It can't be said too often: *The False Core-False Self is not you.* This is why acting out of an assumed identity leaves you alienated, lonely, misunderstood, and feeling bad in relationship. The only way to really feel unity with another is **ESSENCE** to **ESSENCE** or **I AM** to **I AM**. In order to do this, we must first discover and dismantle our False Self, our compensating identities, and our False Core driver.

THE DYNAMICS OF THE FALSE CORE–FALSE SELF

Though the False Core solidifies during the shock of the Realization of Separation, prior to this, it existed in a latent form. It appears to have an energetic-genetic proclivity, which runs in families, such as cancer, diabetes or heart disease,. There is no choice involved because that would imply you can choose your own genetic proclivities. The very idea of such a choice is narcissistic and reflects the infantile grandiosity behind such statements as, "I create it all," "I chose my parents," "I am responsible for everything."

This energetic-genetic predisposition can be likened to what Homeopathic medicine calls a *miasm*. If your grandfather had tuberculosis, for example, then you would have a proclivity toward that disease though your symptoms might only be a runny nose when it rains. Homeopathic doctors would connect the link by analyzing your genetic lineage. In the same way the False Core -False Self has a energetic-genetic lineage.

The False Core-False Self is also called the False Core *Driver*-False Self *Compensator*. This emphasizes their distinct roles, namely, that the False Core **drives** your psychology while the False Self tries to **compensate** for this false conclusion which perceives this conclusion is you.

In a very simple way, we can say that on a neurological level, the brain organizes in the following order: 1) There is a bodily sensation. 2) Another part of the brain registers and acknowledges the sensation. 3) The sensation is then labeled as sadness, fear, happiness, anger, etc. 4) Then, from another level, the brain says, "Sadness is bad," or "Happiness is good." 5) On yet another level, the brain says, "I should change sadness into happiness, I should do something about it."

Each time you move up a level, you get further away from what *is*. You move away from your basic sensation, which is what is, to the cortical level of your brain, which is defining what it is. In other words, as you move from the level of sensation (1) to sadness (3), millions of stimuli are *omitted* and a few are *selected out* by the nervous system and brain to draw this particular conclusion. In this way, you move further away from *what is*, as the nervous system chooses what information to use and draws more conclusions about why what is, is. Furthermore, the labeling of sensation occurs after the experience has already happened, and the nervous system's label omits and selects out so much information, and it only justifies, thus coming up with reasons about what is, which are untrue. The False Core conclusion, therefore, since it omits so much more than it takes in, is not even close to what really is. It is a map, an idea of what is—not what is.

In this way, Alfred Korzybski, the noted father of general semantics said, "The map is not the territory," "the idea is not the thing it is referring to."

HOW DOES THE FALSE CORE-FALSE SELF FUNCTION IN RELATIONSHIP?

Your False Core-False Self is a lens, a trance, through which you view the world, you view your relationship, you view yourself, and also how you imagine the world and your partner views you. In this way, the False Core of, say, "I am worthless" or "I am inadequate," will interpret every relationship situation through this lens or trance.

Each False Core-False Self interprets relationships through its own particular lens. If four people are in an intimate relationship and there is a break up, one might say, "I'm worthless, that's why it happened." Another might feel a deep sense of powerlessness and still a third might feel, "What's wrong with me? I should have been more perfect, loving, connecting," etc. In other words, each False Core has interpreted the same trauma through three different lenses and gives three different reasons, stories, or justifications for the relationship ending. If you could take off the lens, if you could dismantle the False Core, you would feel the ease and flow of life and be able to resonate with another from **ESSENCE** and the **I AM**.

To take this a step further, I am often asked, "Why are **ESSENCE** and **I AM** not available in a relationship?" The reason they go unnoticed or are not stabilized in our awareness is because most of our attention is focused on the False Core. At the same time we are continually trying to somehow overcome it through the False Self Compensator. It should be noted that vulnerability, intimacy, and merger are desired aims in relationship and yet can trigger the shock of the Realization of Separation and the False Core. Any attempt to reform the False Core, transform it, reframe it, re-associate it, take the good or healthy stuff, and leave the bad unhealthy stuff, turn our vices into virtues, etc.—all are strategies of the False Self Compensator which tries to overcome, resist and resolve the False Core. As you can see, the False Self can be extremely insidious. Also, it is important to remember that the False Core-False Self is one holographic unit; you can't have one without the other.

The False Core always wins, it always re-enforces itself. In other words, if your False Core is "I am worthless," "I am unlovable," no matter how much you give to another in relationship to try to feel a sense of worth or love, deep down you always feel worthless and unloved and unlovable. Why? Because it is the False Self doing the giving to get love or worth. So it is the False Self giving to get and overcoming the False Core.

If your False Core is "I am inadequate," no matter how much you try to prove how adequate you are, deep down you still feel inadequate. What compounds the problem is that **ESSENCE** and the **I AM** become involved in the shock and get mixed together with the False Core. After the shock of the Realization of Separation trauma, you conclude that it was caused by **ESSENCE-I AM**, which is then mis-labeled, and its essential quality of **spaciousness** is now seen as emptiness, as a lack.

And so we deny and resist our **ESSENCE-I AM** (the Stateless State) because it is fused with the shock of the Realization of Separation and the False Core, and thus we blame and want to get rid of it. In order to grow the awareness of **ESSENCE,** it requires freeing up the awareness which is unknowingly fixated on the False Core-False Self. Once we realize that the False Core-False Self is an attempt to organize and resist the chaos resulting from the shock of the Realization of Separation, and are willing to go through that, our narcissistic wound begins to heal, everything shifts, our fixation on the False Core-False Self begins to soften, **ESSENCE-I AM** moves into our awareness, and our *relationship expectations of the other soften*. This is a major awakening in relationships.

17

Because of the False Core, results in therapy are often poor since you are trying to heal a false reason, a false story which was made-up by the nervous system to justify and organize the shock of the Realization of Separation. Furthermore, the False Self is oftentimes re-enforced in therapy as it is strengthened to resist the False Core. "Therapy" is sometimes centered around creating a False Self Compensator or acting "as if," or even pretending, an attempt to hide, overcome, resist, heal, or transform a mistaken, infantile conclusion about the shock of the Realization of Separation. In this process, **ESSENCE** is denied while, ironically, at the same time, the False Self is constantly searching for it as a solution to the problem. This searching only re-enforces the False Core-False Self, which needs to be experienced as false in order for **ESSENCE-I AM** to be realized and the shock of the Realization of Separation to be gone beyond.

If the trance of the False Core-False Self does not end, it will continue to be acted out in relationship.

THREE POINTS TO REMEMBER

Point 1: The first False Core identity is the strongest. Let's say "I am unlovable" is the first identity. A person will continually attempt to prove his or her lovingness or lovability to overcome lovelessness. But nothing can be overcome by the False Self because all attempts to prove love are driven by lovelessness. For this reason, no matter how many times the person succeeds in life—deep down, they feel bad about themselves.

Point 2: You, the **I AM**, were there *prior* to any identities. And while the identity called "loveless" is there and after it leaves, the same **I AM** is and will be there. Therefore, you cannot be your identities. Often in therapy, to get a client to appreciate that they were there prior to their identity, I say to them, "Tell me the difference between you and this image, feeling or thought called *fill in the blank*."

Point 3: The "I" you call "you" is part of the False Core-False Self complex. When it disappears there is No "I". My teacher in India, Nisargadatta Maharaj, used to say, "Who came first, you or this 'I' (*I-dentity*)?"

UNCOOKED SEEDS IN RELATIONSHIP

In India, some gurus use the metaphor of seeds. If I have seeds and I plant and water them, I will soon have a plant which bears fruit. But if I first cook the seeds in a frying pan and then plant them, they won't grow or bear fruit. In this scenario, the seeds are symbols of your unprocessed, undigested psychological material, the False Core-False Self. Awareness is the heat that cooks uncooked seeds (repressed, unprocessed) concepts. Thus, we use awareness to cook the uncooked seeds (beliefs, concepts, points of view, etc.) so that they no longer sprout and **ESSENCE-I AM** can become more available in relationship because attention is no longer unknowingly placed upon them. Unfortunately, with each new external context a different aspect of our False Core (uncooked seeds) can emerge. To illustrate this, take for example, a person who is not in relationship. They are pretty content, their work is okay. Soon they meet someone and the external context of their life changes as it gets sexual, what happens next? All their uncooked seeds (stuff) sprouts.

RELATIONSHIP PRINCIPLE:

As the external context changes, different parts of your uncooked seeds (False Core) arise.

SOME EXAMPLES OF
DIFFERENT FALSE CORES

Let us now look at all of this through the eyes of different False Core Drivers and False Self Compensators.

Let's say at age forty, a relationship ends.

One False Core would say, "There's something wrong with me, that's the reason this happened."

Another False Core would say, "I'm worthless, even my partner is treating me as if I'm worthless.

Another False Core would probably get totally frozen and be unable to do anything about it.

Another False Core would say, "I'm getting divorced and it really means I'm incredibly inadequate. It's my own fault, I screwed up."

Another False Core would dissociate. "After all, I'm nothing, I have nothing, I don't even exist, Maybe nothing happened." They have split off from the emotional dimension associated with the event.

Another False Core might think, "This means I will be alone forever."

Another False Core might say, "I'm incomplete, I'm not enough. If only I were enough, had more experiences, then it wouldn't have happened."

Another False Core might feel powerless. Interestingly, the "I am powerless" False Cores often might resist this by saying, "Actually I decided to leave him/her—it was my idea, even though it was the "other."

Another False Core might say, "See, I knew there was no love in the world, and I am unlovable."

THE MAJOR FALSE CORE-FALSE SELVES

Following is a list of the major False Core-False Selves. There might be a tendency to jump in and say, "This is me" or "That is definitely not what I do." But it takes time to figure out your False Core-False Self since often it's what you don't know which actually drives your psychology, as opposed to what you do know.

FALSE CORE	FALSE SELF
1. "Something is wrong with me."	Prove that I am perfect.
2. "I am worthless."	Prove that I have value or worth.
3 . "I cannot do."	Prove that I am an achiever.
✓4. "I am inadequate."	Prove that I am adequate
5. "I don't exist."	Prove that I exist or am something.
6. "I am alone."	Prove that I am connected.
7. "I am incomplete."	Prove that I feel complete.
8. "I am powerless."	Prove that I am powerful.
9. "I am loveless."	Prove that I am lovable.

HEALING THE FALSE CORE-FALSE SELF: WHO IS IN THE DRIVER'S SEAT?

You have to be willing to look at and acknowledge everything that is there. Or as Nisargadatta Maharaj said, "You cannot let go of something until you know what it is." Without dismantling the False Core-False Self, you can only expect to re-live it in your *intimate relationships*.

> RELATIONSHIP PRINCIPLE:
>
> The more intimate the relationship, the higher the probability of activating or triggering your False Core-False Self.

In the process of going beyond the False Core-False Self, the False Self tries to overcome the False Core and the False Cause's reason for the shock—which is not the shock itself. Most attempts to heal or transform the False Core re-enforce it because it is still an attempt to overcome or compensate for it. The False Self is part of the False Core, it appears later than the False Core and hence, it is more false than the False Core. It is the False Self which tries to overcome the False

21

Core. Why is the False Self unable to heal or overcome the False Core? The False Core-False Self is one unit, like inhaling and exhaling, and you can't have one without the other. That's why I prefer the descriptions of each False Core-False Self to focus on the False Core since it is less compensated, closer to the experience, and demonstrates that which drives the machinery of your psychology.

Some psychological schools believe that the False Self Compensator is healthier than the False Core. In this relationship psychology, however, we feel the opposite is true, that the compensator only gives the illusion of being healthier or more socially acceptable, but in reality it is an age-regression, insidiously using the False Self as a defense against the False Core and the Realization of Separation. Until the False Self mask and image, and its seductive, insidious nature is understood as an illusion, and an integrated age regression—and the discomfort felt and gone through—it is impossible to dismantle the False Core-False Self structrue.

People respond to the False Core through the False Self by saying, "If only I didn't feel *fill in the blank*, everything would be fine." In this way they are always trying to get rid of the False Core by over compensation. For example, in order to handle the *fill in the blank*, "I'll take another lover. I'll make more money and then I won't be *fill in the blank*. If I have more experiences, then I'll be smart enough and I won't feel *fill in the blank*." These attempts to get rid of it, heal it, and transform it, are done by the False Self, and they only reenforce the False Core, rather than just noticing, "Hey, here's my False Core of *fill in the blank*, isn't that interesting? I've organized my whole life around a concept which is not true!" If you can do this, you will soon see that it is only a concept—and an untrue concept at that.

Next, study it and dismantle it until it can begin to fall away. You might see it, observe the associations, tracing back every thought, feeling and fantasy to see how your whole life

has been organized around this one thing, and then dismantling it through enquiry. Ultimately, the enquiry continues until
you realize that you are neither the enquirer, the questioner
nor the answerer. But this understanding occurs much after
you see how everything is organized around this one structure. It is then that you can go beyond the obsessive-compulsive nature of the conceptual structure of the False Core, thus
liberating your awareness.

Many therapeutic schools attempt to deal with the False
Core by saying that it can be overcome, healed or transformed.
In doing so, they merely appeal to the seeker's False Self.
These systems wind up creating spiritualized Archetypical
stories, such as the fall of man, to explain and justify what is
a natural, biological separation process—the shock of the
Realization of Separation. It's not that these systems are, by
their nature, bad; but they can re-enforce the False Core-False
Self dynamic within relationships.

Many people are confused about "What is driving their
psychology? What is the one concept that organizes everything in your life?" In relationship, you must understand and
become clear about the False Core, and then trace all of your
behavior back to it. This is an internal process, tracing your
behavior, your actions, your feelings—in short, everything—
back to your False Core. Once you get there, you will have to
sit in it. There's no way around it. Do not try to change it.
Anytime you try to change it or get rid of it, you are resisting
it, which is one of the five strategies, or the five R's, of the
False Self, namely, *re*-sisting, *re*-enacting, *re*-creating, *re*-
enforcing and *re*-solving.

You must be willing to sit in your False Core and the
shock of the Realization of Separation. Sitting in your False
Core means you are free to and free not to BE or UN-BE it,
but not to believe it, just to observe it *without trying to get rid
of it*. Then, to go beyond it, you learn to be able to stay in the
non-verbal **I AM** level prior to it.

As I said previously, every movement of your mind is driven by the False Core, and the interplay of the False Core-False Self. To paraphrase Nisargadatta Maharaj, Notice the ongoing contradictions within the mind (which is the False Core-False Self) and know they are not you. The movements of the mind are done to avoid the pain of the shock of the Realization of Separation and the False Core, which act as a False Cause, thus giving the False Self something to overcome. But since the fantasized cause, or False Core reason, for the Realization of Separation is false, its solution too must be false. In this way *the False Core-False Self deprives you of the experience of deepening your relationships*. Its obsessive-compulsive nature eats away at your perception and avoids awareness of the **ESSENCE and I AM**, which are blamed for the separation, and in the end create relationships based on the Realization of Separation and the False Core-False Self.

Once you understand this, you can begin to trace everything back from the False Self to the False Core and stay there until it dissolves.

THE FALSE CORE-FALSE SELF ENQUIRY

This might help to explain how this tracing process might proceed: Let's say I'm in my room in Oakland and I have a fantasy that me and my partner will be more affectionate or communicative. I ask myself, *If this doesn't come true, what would be the worst of it? Or what's so bad about that?* "Well, the worst part about him not being affectionate, or communicating more, is that I feel empty. Like I don't get what I want." Then, I would continue with my enquiry: "So what's the worst part or what's so bad about feeling empty or like I don't ever get what I want?" I might respond, "Well no one would seem to have anything to do with me and I would feel alone." Continue the enquiry. Question: *"What's the worst of being alone?"* Response: "Well, I feel like I have no love." Enquiry question: *"What's the worst of having no love?"* Response: *"That's it!"* The enquiry continues until you reach bottom where ultimately you'd get, *"That's it!"*

Once you know what you're False Core is, you'll see that every fantasy you have—good, bad or indifferent—and everything that you're doing, can be traced back to your False Core. What makes it so difficult to get the False Core? Because between the False Core and the False Self there's a layer of amnesia which prevents the False Self knowing about the False Core. But fortunately for us, no trance and no amnesia are fool-proof so the False Core is always leaking through. Thus, the False Self can never overcome the False Core, no matter what techniques the False Self uses. The problem is that attempts to transform the False Core actually play into the hands of the False Self, which is doing the work. A few years ago a man came to one of my False Core-False Self workshops. He said that he realized "I was still taking this workshop and learning these techniques so that I could *connect* better and not be alone." Another problem is that the False Self is very tricky, so tricky, in fact, that you actually don't realize what's happening. You're seduced into believing that this time things are going to come out differently (and you will overcome the False Core); but, of course, everything always winds up exactly the same.

GOING BEYOND THE FALSE CORE
The False Core Deconstruction Process

Step 1. Acknowledge that there is a False Core-False Self.
Step 2. Own it.
Step 3. Un-own it. Get that it's not you.

Does the False Core Come Back after it is Worked-Out?

The answer is yes, under stress the False Core will come back. But as you become familiar with it, you will realize it and immediately discard it rather than acting it out. A student once asked my teacher, Nisargadatta Maharaj, "Does anything ever come up for you?" "Every so often something comes up," he said, "but I *immediately* realize it's not me and discard it." So, it's important to be able to trace every thought, emotion, and fantasy, back to its source, the False Core.

How to Work with the False Core-False Self

As mentioned before, the False Self comes into being as a defense against the False Core. That's the bad news. The good news is that you're not either of them. You're not your False Core or your False Self. They're just constructs, made-up concepts. Unfortunately, most people believe they're real, and they think that's who they are. But think of it like this: Before you took on your False Core, you were there in what was a no-state state—a Stateless State of no thoughts, memory, emotion, associations or perceptions. When you dismantle your False Core and it leaves, you will still be there. So, therefore, you can't be your False Core-False Self because when it is gone, the **I AM** is still there.

Notice any experience or thought that you're having right now. Now, prior to taking on that thought, simply stay there. The reason the False Core is so powerful is because all of your awareness and attention is unknowingly fixated on it. And you're always trying to overcome it.

As long as the False Core-False Self is operative, awareness in **ESSENCE-I AM** can never stabilize, and as long as the False Core-False Self is operative, *intimate relationships* become the battleground for their on-going re-enactment.

> RELATIONSHIP PRINCIPLE:
> Who you are is beyond the way you fixate your attention. The way you fixate attention, and all you call *you*, are part of the observer-False Core Driver-False Self Compensator Defensive complex.

TRAUMAS

The False Core has an associational component which acts like a filter through which all traumas are perceived, ordered and experienced. These traumas are then generalized to interpret different externals in order to reinforce and justify itself and what is happening. Thus, the False Core-False Self acts as a lens of interpretation. If your parents were separated at an early age and you developed the False Core of "Nobody loves me," then this interpretation of that experience and what it means to you will be used to interpret all subsequent relationship experiences throughout your life.

In traumas especially there is a collapsing and confusing of the levels. Prior to trauma, everything is in motion—thoughts, memories, sensations, emotions, and body movements. In fact, to have any experience, neurons of the nervous system must move. But when a trauma occurs, three things happen: 1) Motion ceases; 2) memory freezes; and 3) the levels collapse. At this point, our nervous system's survival mechanism produces a survival response of, "I will not let this happen again." A scanning-searching device is created which seeks out real or imagined danger to make sure it won't, and a fight or fright response is evoked if it appears that it might. But as you know by now, most of these responses are in past time, hence, they are inaccurate, and since the experience is resisted, there is an obsessive compulsive tendency to right the wrong, by recreating the same pattern again and again. Freud called this *repetition-compulsion*. In this way, we re-live the same relationship pattern again and again.

As far as collapsing the levels, when traumas are obsessively-compulsively relived, the following happens:

1. The levels (see Chapter VI) are frozen, causing a picture memory to be formed.

2. The picture memory creates an obsessive-compulsive tendency to relive the pain as a way to try and right the wrong.

3. Since the frozen memory is unpleasant it re-enforces the False Core driver.

AMNESIA

Tracing your False Core requires that you see the relationship between your False Core Driver and your False Self Compensator, and how they interact within the context of your *intimate relationship*. This normally cannot be done because there is a layer of **amnesia**, which separates the False Core from the False Self and which prevents you from knowing that they are related.

Since the False Core is so completely defended, all unwanted experiences are relegated to it. The False Core-False Self remains as one holographic unit unknowingly fused together by the associational trance until the trance of the False Core-False Self is broken.

SOME STEPS TOWARD DISMANTLING THE FALSE CORE-FALSE SELF

Step I: Trace your experience back to the False Core Driver.

Step II: Notice where the I-dentity is located in your body at the present time.

Step III: Notice the I-dentity's size and shape.

Step IV: Take the label off the I-dentity. Have it as energy.

Step V: Allow the I-dentity as energy to move from the present time body to another physical location in the room, i.e., externalize it.

Step VI: Acknowledge, own, and observe the False Core-False Self in your *intimate relationship*.

Step VII: Un-own the False Core. This means "getting" that the False Core-False Self is not you. UN-BE the False Core-False Self.

SUMMARY

The False Core-False Self drives problems within *intimate relationships*.

So again, the the False Core is the one belief, concept, idea or conclusion which is identified with and which is both the organizer and driver of all your chains of thoughts, emotions, fantasies, actions, reactions, associations, and relationships.

For this reason it can be said, that the False Core *pulls your chain*.

And why is it called the False Core? Because it was a False assumption, from the point of view of an infant, which was (and is) based on a False conclusion. It is *core* because it forms the *core* of your psycho-emotional and *intimate relationship* life.

There's good news, however. Below your False Core lies your **ESSENTIAL** core and the **I AM**, and the possibility of intimate relationships.

You do your thing
and I do mine.
I am not here to live up to your *expectations*.
You are not here to live up to mine.
You are you and I am me,
and if by chance we find each other it's beautiful,
and if not, it can't be helped.

Fritz Perls, M.D.

THREE

UNREALISTIC *EXPECTATIONS*

Upon beginning the process of writing about *intimate relationships*, and why they do and do not work, it became pristinely clear that the real issue, the real problem, in relationships could be summarized in two words: **UNREALISTIC *EXPECTATIONS*.** Before we discuss what these unrealistic expectations are, let's first explore what might be the major reason for their existence.

We will begin by stating right up front that, first and foremost, we must acknowledge that we are human beings, as are the people we are in a relationship with. At first this might seem obvious, almost like "Yeah, right, why even bother to mention it." But as you will begin to see in this book, sometimes we lose sight of our partner as a human being in present time. Why does this occur? Our pain originates with the shock of the Realization of Separation. As the infant fantasizes mom's magical ability to fulfill all of its needs, without having to ask, the infant fantasizes omniscience and omnipotence, hence the term "magical mommy." Since this is not real and cannot happen, the fantasized re-merger is demolished and we resist and reluctantly realize that somehow or other, we will have to survive as separate individuals, while simultaniously we continue to hold out the wish of re-merger.

This can be terrifying, and an all-out attempt is made by infants to merge again through mirroring mom, by becoming what she wants them to be, or getting her to mirror them back. Of course, it is all quite unsuccessful.

But still, the infant, now an adult wants *magical mommy* to merge with and take away the pain. Years later, we unconsciously have this unrealistic expectation in our *intimate relationships*, and when it doesn't happen problems start.

This ongoing process of *expectation of merger* through mirroring a partner in hopes that the partner will mirror/merge back, and the difficulties that occur because this must inevitably be unsuccessful, leaves us with our pain. And this is at the root of *intimate relationship* problems. In other words, there is a problem when we *expect* our partners to be magical, fulfilling our needs (sometimes even without our having to ask), and merging with us to avoid separation—but we are getting ahead of ourselves. Where then are these *expectations* rooted? These unrealistic expectations are rooted in the sudden Realization of Separation which feels like a shock as infants realize they are separate from their mother.

This natural separation process leaves the infant with a deep wound. When this wound and shock are not acknowledged and digested, they can have a profound effect on our entire lives. It can leave us with an existential anxiety about our well-being, our ability to survive, and *unrealistic expectations* about our *intimate relationships*, i.e., how to get the other person to help us survive and merge better. Decades later, this separation from mom is projected onto others. We pursue *intimate relationships* unconsciously *expecting* that the other person will take away our separation pain, which is the cause of our False Core.

Simply stated, the *unrealistic expectations* of merger or re-merger, through trying to mind-read another and mirror or match them with the unconscious expectation of merger, is age-regressed and a "pretend" or "act." This mask of the three *M's (me's), of match, mirror, meet,* is only really about the infant's *me,* and enhances relationship pain as it gets originally triggered by the Realization of Separation and later by smaller realizations of separation. It is through this resistance to the Realization of Separation and the attempted *expectation* to get others to merge with us that the False Self, with its innumerable techniques and strategies, dominates our *intimate relationships.*

NOBODY CAN HEAL YOUR
SEPARATION PAIN.

Stephen H. Wolinsky

It is our desire for merger and resistance to separation which hides the wound and represent a basic issue in relationships, namely, our *expectation* that it is the other's (mom) job or responsibility to take away our Separation shock and pain through merger with us.

But why does this implicit *expectation* override our present-time common sense? Because this implicit expectation or *merger wish* is pre-verbal and exists prior to the infant's thought processes, it is not in present time, and hence prior to our common sense. Since it is rooted so deeply in our earliest infancy, this implicit expectation dominates us at our most primitive, psychological level. It dominates us biologically because an infant's survival is dependent on mom taking away our pain, namely, dealing with our hunger, thirst, need for sleep, etc. It dominates us psychologically because we confuse and substitute levels and dimensions for one another since merger is the name of the game, and going for it in any level or way available, is survival. Like a rat in a maze, we will go down the tunnel in hopes of getting cheese. However, unfortunately, we keep going down the same tunnel (relationship) even though there is no cheese there. In this way both *in* and *out of* the therapy office, I have heard many people say, "I just want him [or her] to take care of me." Thus, our desire for merger and resistance to separation forms the False Core-False Self and represents our view of ourselves, and how we imagine the world views us.

CONCLUSION

Unrealistic *expectations* that the *other* in our *intimate relationship* will take away our pain through merger, is rooted in the shock of the Realization of Separation from mom. If this remains unacknowledged, the rest of our lives might be spent trying to merge with another person, with a teacher, guru, or even with God, to overcome the pain of separation.

In practical terms, how does this apply to *intimate relationships*? Well, this *expectation* is first triggered when we fall in love and oftentimes experience the bliss of merger. Unfortunately, as we all have experienced, we soon *get* that we are separate and, as the bliss of merger decreases, our separation realization increases along with our existential angst. Simply put, the bliss of merger oftentimes rooted in early infancy becomes the pain (piss) of separation which then *begets*, in our *intimate relationships*, how do we get to merger again?

THE CHANGE MECHANISM IS AN
AUTOMATIC RESPONSE OF THE NERVOUS
SYSTEM WHEREBY EXTERNAL
CIRCUMSTANCES, OR THE "OTHER,"
ARE BELIEVED TO HAVE
CAUSED AND BE THE SOURCE OF
OUR PAIN. THIS LEADS TO THE
EXPECTATION IN RELATIONSHIP THAT
IF ONLY THE OTHER PERSON CHANGES
AND BEHAVES DIFFERENTLY, THAN "I"
WILL BECOME—PAIN FREE.

Stephen H. Wolinsky

FOUR

THE CHANGE MECHANISM:
THE EXPECTATION OF MERGER

THE CHANGE MECHANISM

The change mechansim is an automatic survival mechanism whereby our pain is imagined to come from *outside* of ourselves. The change mechanism operates and contains three component parts: 1) *The other is the source of my pain and 2) if the other were only different, or changed in some way, my pain would go away, Or 3) if I could change in some way, and be what I imagine they want me to be—then my separation pain would disappear*. Why doesn't it work? Because the *other* is not seen as a present time person but unconsciously as a *past-time* mother with magical, omniscient, omnipotent qualities. We then imagine that *they* will be just like mom (is, was, should be, or wish she were), and take away all of our pain and comfort us, and then we will be merged again. Thus, the *unrealistic expectation* becomes a *Christmas list* of wants which is what we imagine we need from others and from the world to be happy (merged). Looking for others to take care of us or change so we do not feel our False Core reminds me of what the father of Gestalt Therapy, Fritz Perls, said, "Maturity is the movement from environmental support to self-support."

The change mechanism can be simply explained as: I feel separation pain or False Core pain—it must be because of you, or something you are, something that you lack or are not, or something you did or did not do. I then *expect* you to give me what I want, or I *expect* you to merge with me so I don't feel separate (False Core pain). Or if I change in some way, you will want to merge with me and my pain will go away. (Don't confuse this with alcoholic or abusive relationships where a person's pain is *due to* another's behavior.) If separation is explored honestly in *present time*, you can choose to stay in a relationship or not rather than recreating a *past-time* situation of, "I *have* to stay," "I *have* to get you to change," "I suffer because you don't merge with me." Oftentimes, when merger does not occur the messenger of "no merger" is blamed and subtle rage ensues. Even more subtle than "kill the messenger" (partner) who does not merge is blaming the other by diagnosing them as being bad or wrong (or with some psychological diagnosis), which is then used too justify why they are as they are and you are not getting what you want and are in (separation) pain in some way.

This style of killing another I call *death by diagnosis.* Death through diagnosis is the covert way of killing and blaming another because they are the messenger of separation. This process is deeply rooted in the most primitive part of our brain stem. And though now clearly hidden and masked, by societal rules, it could look like, "You are the source of my pain, and my survival is dependent upon my killing (diagnosing) you in some way." One angry client I had was married to a psychologist who was constantly diagnosing him. He looked at her, as her subtle separation anger was leaking through, and said, "So, what's my diagnosis today?" In this way, he was diagnosed as bad or wrong in some way, as separation—either real or imagined—continued to trigger her pain of separation and the change mechanism.

To illustrate, if you don't like a movie that I do, or if you enjoy different kinds of food, then automatically I begin to feel the pain of separation and want to discuss it as some kind of problem (yours), that I feel separate/False Core. But this is *past time* pain. On the other hand, I have not seen you for two weeks and miss you—that is present time pain. Please note that in the first instance, there is an implicit demand that you change and an expectation that my pain is your problem. In the second example, it exists in *present time, with no expectations* that you change so that merger occurs to avoid separation pain.

We all have *expectations*, i.e., I expect you to give me what I want and if you don't, I imagine I'll feel pain. But oftentimes your not giving me what I want triggers my sense of being separate, which in turn activates the shock and my False Core-False Self. And in *intimate relationships* if I feel separate I *assume* it is because you did not give me what I wanted. In this way my covert implicit *expectation* of you is that you will change and handle my pain. Of course, this is not "logical" because it is in *past-time*; but somehow, even though I was in pain before we met, once the change mechanism gets triggered and kicks in, the mantra becomes, "If you change, my pain will go away." Or if I become what I think you want me to be, you will merge with me and my separation pain will disappear. Of course, all of this is not done consciously or deliberately because it is really outside of our awareness.

Naturally, we all know that it doesn't work when we try to make others change or expect them to. But because all of this is pre-verbal and so early, *expectations* continue to escalate as relationships deteriorate. Why? Because even if I change and meet your *expectations*, like a high jumper in the Olympics, the bar is always raised. Why? Because I am separate from you, and your being a certain way can never be enough to handle your unrealistic primitive fantasies and *expectations* of re-merger.

And why does it work out this way? Because to resist the pain of the shock of the Realization of Separation, the change mechanism insists that *you* change so that I can merge again and be free from pain. Or as one of my clients, a married man, once said to his wife, "I can never change enough to satisfy you."

REALIZING YOUR HUMANNESS

When a person in an *intimate relationship* desperately desires merger, many problems arise. Most common occurs when infantile merger causes a loss of boundary of separation. When this occurs, the person cannot tell where their problem ends and their partner's begins. Furthermore, since their pain of separation is so easily ignited, they are in a constant, ongoing state of nervousness and fear. To illustrate, in one couple I saw, the wife, even after years of marriage, constantly asked her husband, "Are you going to leave me?" "You're not going to leave me, are you?"

This conveyed her fear of separation, loss, abandonment, and pain. So, much to his chagrin, whenever she felt separate and in pain, she wanted to "work out the relationship dynamic," as if it had something to do with him rather than being her problem. When he was not interested in this communication, he was labeled and diagnosed in a derogatory way, a poor communicator, etc. She even kept on enrolling him in workshops and classes, in order to help him "be better" in some way so that she did not feel pain.

In this way, she had made *her* problem *his* problem and attempted to get him to change, so she would not have to feel her pain. Unfortunately, she did not realize that her pain was her own problem and that it had nothing to do with him.

In *The Way of the Human* trilogy, I have written that we must first realize our humanness. But how can we when we are in *past-time,* wanting others to change so that we can merge and be out of pain. A Quantum Psychology trainer once said to me, "How do you know when you are finished with your parents? I said "When you realize they are human." In this way realizing your partner is a human being is essential. Once this occurs an essential quality of **ESSENCE**, which is *acceptance*, is realized. Acceptance is not part of the dichotomy of rejection. Acceptance is an essential aspect and quality of **ESSENCE** realizable when you "get" you are a human and so is your partner.

In this way *unrealistic expectations* first must be traced back to our shock of separation, and back to its source. For example, let's say your partner wants to go to the movies and you want to work. A little, almost baby-like electric shock occurs. That shock is a signal that began with the *past-time* BIG SHOCK. Little shocks can be used as signals which can lead us back to the Realization of Separation.

ONCE YOU CAN SEE THE OTHER IN
PRESENT TIME AS A HUMAN BEING,
EXPECTATIONS WILL DIMINISH AND
THE ESSENTIAL QUALITY OF
ACCEPTANCE INCREASE.
ACCEPTANCE IS NOT A
PSYCHOLOGICAL QUALITY.
ACCEPTANCE IS AN ESSENTIAL
QUALITY WHICH ARISES WHEN
YOUR HUMANNESS AND THAT OF
OTHERS IS REALIZED. ONCE THIS
OCCURS YOU EXPERIENCE
ACCEPTANCE WHICH IS LOVE.

Stephen H. Wolinsky

WHY ARE *EXPECTATIONS* UNREALISTIC?

I have met many people who are looking for a relationship. Unfortunately, their *expectations* of the pain of unmet past-time merger, confuses *present-time* reality with past-time reality. For example, recently, when I ask people, "What do you want (in relationship)?" they pull out their *Christmas list*: "I want a man/woman with money," "I want a man/woman who is spiritual," "I want a man/woman who communicates," etc. I recently met a woman from Sweden who had on her *Christmas list*, "And if he could play Chopin—that would be it." This ongoing problem of unrealistic *expectations* (brings the unconscious *past-time* idea that this will bring merger and I'll be out of pain) has created so many wants that a wedge has been driven between men and women.

Christmas lists which Divide Men from Women:

For women with *expectations* unmet	For men with *expectations* unmet
Women are in touch, men are not	Women want too much, men do not
Woman can feel, men do not	Women want us to take care of them,
Woman want intimacy, men do not.	For women it is never enough.
Women want to communicate, men do not	It's always something with women,
	I don't want to be hassled.

CONCLUSION

Because of unrealistic *expectations* based on over-coming the shock of the Realization of Separation, these age-regressed *Christmas lists* get created and escalate. Unfortunately, in process not only does the "other" as a human being get lost in *present-time*, but soon so too does the possibility of having an *intimate relationship*.

ANY ATTEMPT TO CHANGE
ANOTHER, SO THAT THEY
MATCH YOUR IMAGE OF WHO
THEY SHOULD BE SO THAT YOU DO
NOT HAVE TO FEEL YOUR PAIN OF
SEPARATION, IS GRANDIOSE,
NARCISSISTIC, AND WORSE YET,
DEPRIVES YOU AND THE OTHER OF
HIS OR HER HUMANNESS. AND AN
OPPORTUNITY OF VULNERABILITY
AND INTIMACY.

Stephen H. Wolinsky

FIVE

WHERE DOES THAT LEAD US?

Now that we have discussed what the problem is, and where it comes from, we can "begin the beguine."

For many of us, infantile separation is an obtuse, abstract, concept but this book was not intended as a treatise on the details of long-term psychotherapy. Rather, its purpose was to: 1) offer a here-and-now discussion of what the problem is; 2) explore how the problem affects your life; 3) trace behaviors and little shocks back to the BIG SHOCK and how to acknowledge it; 4) how not to step in the shit again; 5) how to look at it honestly and realistically; and 6) how to map out where you are and where it leaves you. Hopefully, this will take us to the place of seeing, knowing, and feeling what the problem is in present time, and how to remedy it by questioning the validity of our *expectations*. In this way, we will begin to notice the trigger of separation, acknowledge our humanness, and understand the essential quality of acceptance which equals love.

RELATIONSHIP ARCHETYPES

An Archetype is a pattern which appears to be universal in nature. For example, imagine you are making cookies with a cookie cutter. Each cookie will look approximately the same as every other cookie. In this metaphor, the Archetype is the cookie cutter and our relationships are the different cookies. Relationships have cookie cutter patterns. We, in the 20th century, with all of our therapy and communication skills somehow imagine we can change these patterns or that they do not apply to us. We are not saying that change is impossible, we are saying that trying to change another to match your *expectations* with the illusion that it will somehow cure your separation pain is an **ARCHETYPE** for relationships. But it is infantile and, at the risk of sounding harsh, at best a fantasy, and at worst, a narcissistic illusion. Narcissists have two qualities: One, they believe that they are the center of the universe; and that others should be their reflection. And two, they believe that their own pain of separation will be alleviated if I mirror, match, meet, or reflect to another what image the other wants or needs and so the other will merge with them.

Problems in Archetypical relationships have always existed, the only difference being that, unlike thousands of years ago, now in the West, they are no longer covert. Instead, everything is endlessly communicated even if the relationships (cookies) are still not processed (digested) but resisted, thus making us feel nauseated. Recently I was asked, "Why do you use the word digested?" Because like a meal, experiences are digested and assimilated. In other words, experience is like food. When they remain undigested and unprocessed, they cause indigestion (pain). The lack of acceptance of *what is* leads to resistance which causes us to not digest *what is* or the way *people are*. This leads to pain which leads to yet more communication, therapy, sharing, and working on the relationship, to figure out why you are not giving me what I want, which ultimately means not merging with me.

I recently worked with a client who always *expected* her partner to do whatever she wanted without her asking for it. When he didn't comply with something, she said he was mean, self-centered, and unwilling to go deeper. In short, *whenever he was not her mirror reflection or did not match her expectations or the picture of who he should be, he became the problem*, he was the one who had something to work on. To sum it up, she had not digested, accepted or assimilated who her husband was, and was still trying to blame and diagnose him for her being in separation pain. This is like buying a pizza and arguing with the pie that it's not chow mein. First, you try to get the pizza to be chow mein. Then, you analyze the pizza's problem and communicate about the pizza not being chow mein and discuss your feelings. And finally you work with the pizza so that it will taste like chow mein. And guess what? When everything is done, it's still a pizza.

IS THERE A NEED FOR CHANGE?

No, the Archetypes do not need to be changed. In fact, when we try to change them, we only wind up resisting them. What does need to be developed is the ability to: 1) look at our little shocks; 2) trace them to the BIG SHOCK; 3) stay with the shock of the Realization of Separation; 4) don't act out the change mechanism; 5) allow our *essential* qualities of spaciousness, love, and acceptance, which naturally occurs once we go through the separation pain and become aware of the change mechanism, and the False Core-False Self.

THE FALSE CORE-FALSE SELF IN RELATIONSHIP

You are not perfect—I must get you to be perfect.
OR
I am perfect—I can make you perfect.

ETC.

I am worthless—You give me value.
OR
You are worthless—I will give you value.

ETC.

I cannot do anything—You can do it for me.
OR
I can do everything—You can do nothing.

ETC.

You are inadequate—I can make you adequate.
OR
I am adequate— I can make you adequate.

ETC.

You are withdrawn—I can bring you out.
OR
I am withdrawn—You can bring me out.

ETC.

I am alone—I must connect with you.
OR
I am connected—I must teach get you to connect.

ETC.

I am incomplete—You can complete me.
OR
I am complete—I can complete you.

ETC.

I have no power—I want you to give me power.
OR
I am powerful—I can make you powerful.

ETC.

I have no love—You can give me love.
OR
I am loving—I can give you the love you need.

ETC.

THE MAJOR PROBLEM?

Why is the other person or object (such as power, love, material wealth, etc.) *never enough*?

Because when we attempt to *get* in *present time* what was missing in *past time* means that we are not in *present time*. Instead, we are living an infantile illusion, taking past time *expectations* of merger and projecting them onto another person or object in present time in a feeble attempt to get what we needed then—**NOT NOW**. Then, when the other does not mirror or reflect back what we imagine we want—we exhibit infantile rage, blame, and seek a divorce.

NOBODY OUTSIDE OF YOU CAN HEAL YOUR SHOCK OF THE REALIZATION OF SEPARATION AND THE ACCOMPANYING SEPARATION WOUND.

Stephen H. Wolinsky

SIX

THE RELATIONSHIP LEVELS:
THE MAP MADE SIMPLE

WHY A MAP?

First of all, why a map? A map can be a handy thing to have as long as we don't confuse it with the territory; that is, as long as we see it as a diagram or chart. In this way we can see the development of a relationship, where we are and where we are going, and realize that maybe it's time to change trains and let go of the relationship, or at least acknowledge where we are so we can be realistic with ourselves and make realistic decisions.

Or in the words of the late sufi master Idries Shah, "It is silly to wait and hope for a train that is never coming."

So this is what a relationship map does, it gives us a view of the road. This helps us to see where we are and how we got there. It also explains why the trip was difficult. It also helps us to decide if we should stay on the road or call off the trip. Let's begin by taking a look at the map.

THE DIMENSIONS OF MANIFESTATION: AN OVERVIEW

What are the dimensions of manifestation and what do they have to do with relationships? The dimensions of manifestation are the different levels of experience that a human being has and which they relate through and on. As we will explore in this chapter, these dimensions can become confused and substituted when issues of separation and shock enter the picture. First, we will give an overview of these dimensions.

THE DIMENSIONS OF MANIFESTATION MADE EASY

THE EXTERNAL LEVEL: Involving the external world, children, career, living arrangements, etc.

THE THINKING LEVEL: Involving values, beliefs, thoughts, concepts, fantasies, images, etc.

THE EMOTIONAL LEVEL: Involving fear, hope, joy, hate, anger, jealousy, etc.

THE BIOLOGICAL LEVEL: Involving eating, sleeping, sex, learning, etc.

THE ESSENTIAL LEVEL: Involving acceptance unconditional love, forgiveness, compassion, etc.

THE SPIRITUAL LEVEL: Awareness of the consciousness which connects us all, etc.

OUR DESIRE TO MERGE AND TO
RESIST SEPARATION CAUSES US TO
FOCUS ON WHATEVER
DIMENSION IS AVAILABLE FOR
MERGER AND EXCLUDE
OR IGNORE THOSE WHICH ARE
NOT AVAILABLE. THIS LEADS US TO
CONFUSE, IGNORE, AND
ATTEMPT TO OVERCOME OR
SUBSTITUTE ONE DIMENSION
FOR ANOTHER.

Stephen H. Wolinsky

SEVEN

THE EXTERNAL WORLD

THE CONTEXT

Few of us would deny that one of the best ways to meet people is to find someone with similar interests to our own. It is through our external interests that we generally begin our relationships. When I say external or context, I remember watching a show with Dr. Ruth, the one-time famous television psychologist. People would write or call her and say, "I want to meet somebody, where should I go? How can I meet them, I have this terrible time hooking up with people." Her advice was pretty accurate. She would always ask the caller, "What do you like to do? What do you really enjoy as a hobby, or what do you really enjoy doing in your life." The person would generally say something like tennis, going to the theater, or dancing. Dr. Ruth would tell them, "What you should do is go to the theater, go play tennis, go folk dancing, go into areas that are interesting to you where available women and men are, and that's where you'll meet someone. If you're not interested in drinking, smoking or carousing, don't go to bars because the kind of person you're going to meet there is probably going to be someone with vastly different interests than you have. You have to go where your interests are if you want to meet someone."

The first level of relationship usually begins with the external world. The external world is the context in which you live, work and play. What do you like to do? What don't you like to do? What are your life interests? Do you like rock and roll concerts or ballet, films or theater? Do you like playing golf or tennis or just hanging out reading? Do you like bicycling or taking walks? The things you like are your external interests. Each of these activities will be associated with specific places, and they are where you might go if you want to meet someone who has similar interests. Of course, you will meet people generally where you hang out. That seems like logical and obvious advice.

But at the same time, there are so many levels of awareness, as all of us have experienced, that we might go folk dancing or to a tennis club and meet somebody who seems interesting. So, why is it that we might play a wonderful tennis game, but when we sit down afterward, there is nothing to talk about? This happens because, though there is an external relationship, there is really no resonance on any of the other levels. This is an extremely significant discovery because, as I have noticed with my friends as well as myself, that we have not acknowledged all our levels of relationship. And for this reason, you can have external connections with someone but no psychological or emotional connection.

And so, the first level is our context, the externals, actions, the *doing* part of a relationship.

DETERMINING WHERE YOU ARE IN THE EXTERNALS

The External World Explained

The external world is probably the most emphasized of all the areas that people relate to. The external world focuses on what you do, what you like to do and how you are organized. At a workshop I gave recently, one of my friends, who had been happily married for twenty-five years, was sitting there. A bunch of people were talking about why relationships worked and what they wanted and what they did not want. My friend said, "What really matters is, Can you live together? This is probably the most important questions: Can you live together on a functional level?

So at this point, function can be seen as a subset of the external dimension. The external world is concerned with things you like to do whether it's hiking, tennis, taking classes or whatever. On a functional level, the question to ask is, Are you functionally able to live together? Interestingly, the concept of marrying for love is a relatively recent development. Historically speaking, most people did *not* marry for love. In fact, even in Western cultures, until the last 150 years marriages were primarily "arranged," and in India most marriages are still arranged by parents. The parents determine these arrangements based on an external reasons.

In India, for example, the primary reason would be based on the person's caste. Other considerations would be their economic position, educational background, as well as their parents' occupation and their bloodline. These are all factors that determine fixing a marriage. I recently worked with a client who had a Master's degree in Economics and who came from a very wealthy family. She had been married for about eight years to a man from a lower middle class family with not much of an educational background. The marriage was unsuccessful and it did not work for functional reasons. My client wanted more education, she wanted to learn things, do things, expand her horizons, and she liked to travel. Her husband had never gone to college and didn't have much interest as far as academic achievement went. He felt no need to buy a larger house since his needs and wants were much different than hers—not bad or good—just different. Where she wanted to expand and grow, he on the other hand was satisfied with the status quo. Because of these differences, their marriage was always in conflict. If you try to use one level, such as love (essential) or sex (biological) to overcome another level, such as your external differences, you are doing what Relationship Psychology calls, *Confusing the levels*. When you confuse the levels, it oftentimes leads to further relationship problems down the road.

THE SHOCK OF THE REALIZATION
OF SEPARATION YIELDS THE DESIRE
TO RE-MERGE AND OVERCOME
THE SHOCK. SINCE, RARELY, IF
EVER, ARE ALL DIMENSIONS
AVAILABLE FOR AN INFANT TO
MERGE WITH, THEY WILL TAKE
THOSE AVAILABLE AND DISCOUNT
THE OTHERS.

YEARS LATER, THIS BECOMES
AUTOMATIC AND A PSYCHOLOGY
AND PHILOSOPHY WILL EMERGE
TO JUSTIFY, AND/OR TRY TO
°OVERCOME ONE DIMENSION
WITH ANOTHER.

Stephen H. Wolinsky

The external world not only deals with what you like to do, it also deals with background and history. I remember my uncle. After twenty-five years of marriage, his wife died of cancer. A few years later, he married a woman very similar to my aunt. She had children of about the same age, had a similar background, and lived in the same kind of house. Several years later, she also died of cancer also, and he eventually met another woman. It was the same story again—similar age, social economic bracket, children grown up, similar houses, and their spouses had died. What I realized was that even as close as one generation ago, people did not always marry expressly for love but that other factors figured into the match. Love, of course, was there; however, what came first was function. What is function? Function deals with the questions of, What do you do? What do I do? What are our backgrounds? Can we first function together as a unit? If he likes to live in the country and I like the city, that's not functional. If he likes to travel and I like to stay at home, again, it's not functional.

The external world not only deals with whether you like to play tennis or not; but with all of our backgrounds, religion, education, culture, goals, ambitions, finances, family patterns, do you want children? how many? etc. It asks, What are is your basic lifestyle, and can we mesh successfully, or are we sentencing ourselves to years of strain, confusion, and thwarted plans and goals. When people ignore the externals and pay no attention to function, they often wind up in a relationship which doesn't work.

EXTERNAL WORLD—QUESTIONNAIRE
(To be done with your partner or potential partner)

I. <u>Lifestyle</u>
  A. What interests do you have in common?
  B. How much time do you spend on your work?
    a. Less than 20 hours a week
    b. 20—40 hours a week *STUDY - SELF WORK*
    c. 40+ hours a week *2-6 PLACES*
    d. Career or profession does not apply
  C. How much alone time do you need?
    a. very little
    b. some, but not lots
    c. I thrive on it *read*
  D. What do you do when you have time off? *SAME AS B VOLUNTEER*
  E. Are you an on the go type of person, or stay at home type?
  F. What kind of diet do you have?
    a. eat out a lot
    b. health food
    c. gourmet cuisine
    d. all American home cooking
    e. do not pay much attention to it
  G. How clean or messy are you?
    a. meticulous can't function unless it's clean
    b. I like it clean but I only do it when needed
    c. I get the basics done *DO NOT FUNCTION WELL IN DISORDER*
    d. living in chaos is acceptable
  H. What about cigarettes, alcohol, drugs?

II. <u>Economics</u>
  A. What is your current income level?
  B. What was your economic level growing up?

63

    C. Do you bring into the relationship large amounts
       of money orany large debts or financial obliga-
       tions?
    D. How do you (want to) arrange the finances in the
       relationship?
         a. combine everything
       ✗ b. keep each of our money separate
         c. one partner takes on larger proportion
         d. one partner handles all the money
         e. shared responsibility for money
         f. other

III. Children / family

This is a very important topic and you should make an
honest appraisal of how you both feel, especially in the for-
mative stages of a relationship. Often, there will be denial of
your feelings to accommodate your partner's. You may experience a certain self-deception with beliefs such as, "I can
adjust," or "He'll change his mind later." The issue of children and family is a major cause of dissent and incompatibil-
ity in a relationship. For all involved, especially the children,
it is a smart idea to be honest with one's feelings in regards to
what is such a significant undertaking—whether in creating
a new family or in dealing with children from a previous relationship.

    A. What is the current situation with regards to chil-
       dren in each of your lives? If so, how involved a
       parent or stepparent are you?
    B. What are your assumptions, *expectations* and feel-
       ings in regards to being involved with your
       partner's children? With your partner's involve-
       ment with your children?
    C. Do you want to have children together? How strong
       are your feelings about this matter?

IV. <u>Future Vision</u>
  A. Individually or together as a couple, where you want to be in:
    a. 1 year
    b. 3 years
    c. 5 years
  In each of the below areas:
    a. financially
    b professionally
    c. family
    d. spiritually
    e. geographically
    f. socially

V. <u>Time</u>
  A. Make a circle which you will divide into "pie slices," the size of each segment according to time spent in the following areas. Compare with your partner.
    a. work
    b. family
    c. primary relationship
    d. recreation
    e. social, community
    f. physical activity
    g. spiritual
    h. alone time

Hopefully, these questions will enable you to explore how you and your partner relate on each of the external levels. The purpose of the questions was to look for functional compatibility as well as functional differences. Some difference will be easily digested into the relationship. Others may be major issues of contention. How you view your differences may be determining factors of the ease at which you relate to each other through the external and the other levels.

CONCLUSION

Hopefully, this discussion will help you to meet and appreciate someone on an external and functional level. When your levels do not match each other's, it is obviously much more difficult to maintain a long-term relationship. Ignoring function and externals, the lack of similar cultural and historical biases, and no common ground—all of these might explain why you don't get what you want from your intimate relationships.

EIGHT

YOUR INTERNAL THINKING WORLD

The thinking world is involved with our thoughts, beliefs, images, fantasies, and concepts as they relate to the internal world and our external relationships. The thinking and emotional levels are extraordinarily significant in all of our relationships. In order to have a *thoughtful* resonance with someone, it can be important that you *think* along the same lines or have similar values. For example, when it comes to *intimate relationships*—although this is not always the case—you generally don't find somebody in the radical Right with somebody from the radical Left. You usually don't find someone who is pro-life when their partner is pro-choice. Very rarely do you find couples whose thoughts and beliefs about things vary in extremes; there is generally a certain range. On the psychological level, their thought processes and values are reasonably similar and so are their values in relationship.

The thinking world can be extremely confusing for people, given that men are *supposedly* from Mars and women are from Venus. Certainly men and women think differently. Traditional research claims that men are predominately left-brain oriented and tend to think on a more rational, linear level. They have a tendency to analyze everything and draw conclusions. Women, on the other hand, are *supposedly* more right-brain oriented and tend to be more intuitive and more flowing. Accordingly, men see experience in terms of beginnings, middles, and ends, whereas women see things as an on-going process. Because of this *very, very generalized* tendency to think rather than feel, men are less able to relate on a feeling level than women.

In her recent studies, the renowned psychologist Carol Gilligan has questioned the validity of various developmental models of psychology. Gilligan's groundbreaking work showed that one of the reasons men and women are different is because they are brought up differently, rather than men being healthy and women not being as healthy.

In the past, due to biology and cultural baggage, i.e., upbringing, many men are more focused on work and on being analytic, and a majority of women are more focused on relationships. Both of these outlooks yield very different thinking styles. Men are more into action, they have a *doing* thinking style. They are less concerned with their relationships and more focused on problem solving and its outcome. Again, women, with their right-brain orientation, focus more on relationships and community, both of which become a priority. As might be imagined, in relationships these two opposing perspectives tend to clash. They clash because men are more thinking, more focused on *doing* while women are more into relationship process and into *being*, into family and community.

Both of these have such an enormous impact on the thinking style, it is almost unbelievable. For example, if a woman has a problem, they usually see it in terms of relationships. With men, the focus is on, How can I solve it? How can I work this problem out? So in meeting somebody on a thinking level or thinking style, what we have to look at is, what are the different styles and where and how do they meet? In fact, can they meet?

It goes without saying that the left-brain/right-brain dichotomy is not always along gender lines. Often men will be more into feelings and women into having a career and being out in the world. But nevertheless there does seem to be a prepondernace of men viewing reality as rational and solvable, with their eye focused on the goal, and women who feel that the process of life is in relationship. And of course, these different styles can exist in both partners to varying degrees.

ACKNOWLEDGING THE STYLES

The first and most important thing is to acknowledge the different style that your partner has. Is he more of a thinker? Is he more outcome oriented? Is she more relationship oriented? Once you understand which is which and where you fall, it becomes easier to communicate and this can enhance the possibility of joining on what appears to be a different level but one that can definitely be made more functional.

THE THINKING DIMENSION— QUESTIONNAIRE

(To be done with a partner or potential partner)

1. Do you prefer to think things out before taking an action?

2. Do you look at outcomes first and relationships second?

3. Is achieving something more, or less, important in relationship?

4. If your partner's thinking appears irrational, or not linear, do you try to correct it, or do you allow them to be?

5. Are relationships the most important thing to you?

6. When a problem arises, do you see it first in terms of relationship and, second, in terms of a problem to be solved or vice-versa?

7. Do you have a tendency to move more from your emotions rather than your thoughts?

8. In a conflict with your partner, are you willing and able to meet them on a thinking level, and to see both levels simultaneously?

CONCLUSION

In conclusion, if we want to expand our awareness and enhance our ability to relate to other people, we must learn to appreciate their different thinking styles. To appreciate someone's thinking style, first we must understand what ours is. And if we understand ours, then we can understand and appreciate theirs. At that point, the thinking styles can be shared and we can learn to appreciate our partners thinking style or lack of use of the thinking dimension. The thinking dimension is a critical dimension that is important in our relationships and in our reality.

NINE

THE EMOTIONAL DIMENSION

Probably the most misunderstood and volatile area of relationships are the emotions. Emotions, much to the regret of many left-brain adherents, are not rational. Unlike your thoughts, emotions are more difficult to control. In the emotional world, it is the ability to be in touch with feelings which is important—to be in touch, to experience feelings directly, and to communicate them. You can try to rein them in and to use the thinking dimension to dominate the emotional dimension; but we all know that when push comes to shove, the emotional dimension has more power than the thinking dimension.

As a hugh generalization, in contemporary society men frequently try to override the emotional dimension via the thinking dimensions. How often in a relationship has a woman heard a man say, "Well, that's not rationale?" Or a man heard a woman to say, "Well, it doesn't feel right." To expand a relationship, both partners have to acknowledge each dimension equally, the thinking and the emotional. *Very very generally speaking,* Men often acknowledge the thinking dimension first, the emotional dimension second. Whereas women view the emotional dimension first and the thinking dimension second. In both cases, you are being short-sighted. You can't use one dimension to solve the problems of another dimension. So, if you try to dominate the emotional dimension with the thinking dimension or vice-versa, it just doesn't work. In order to have an *intimate relationship*, you have to be able to understand your emotional and thinking states as well, as those of our spouse or partner.

On an emotional level, a successful couple has similar feelings about many different things. For example, I know a couple where one wanted a child and felt very strongly about it, while the other one didn't. The relationship lost its intimacy. It is important to have shared feelings, and it is also necessary to be able to communicate those feelings with your partner. I have met many women whose chief complaint is that their husbands don't understand their feelings. Oftentimes, in therapy women want to communicate with their husbands, but the men have absolutely no idea what their partners are talking about. This leaves the women feeling feel alienated and isolated. In many relationships, there is little emotional joining between the two partners. This means not be able to experience, share, and be available for the other's feelings. The problem is that the inability to relate emotionally is a shock and often-times triggers the past-time shock of the Realization of Separation, which makes emotions escalate. *The past-time escalation is an individual problem NOT a couple's problem. And this must be understood within the context of the couple.* In an ideal world, however, there is a thinking and an emotional joining, and as part of both, a level of communication. This, of course, deals with the ability of being honest about what you are feeling.

THE EMOTIONAL DIMENSION— QUESTIONNAIRE

(To be done with a partner or potential partner)

1. Did your mother have highly charged emotional states which your father found hard to deal with? Write down or verbally communicate your answers until nothing else comes up.

2. What did your father create in response to your mother's emotional states? Write down or verbally communicate your answers until nothing else comes up.

3. Do you consider thinking states more important than emotional states? Write down or verbally communicate your answers until nothing else comes up.

4. Do you see emotions as something to get rid of that aren't really valid and important? Write down or verbally communicate your answers until nothing else comes up.

5. When somebody, like your spouse, gets into heavy emotions, do you have a tendency to disappear or dissociate? Write down or verbally communicate your answers until nothing else comes up.

6. When your spouse gets into a problem with emotions, do you have a tendency to try to get extra rationale? Write down or verbally communicate your answers until nothing else comes up.

7. Do you suffer from trying to override thoughts with feelings? Write down or verbally communicate your answers until nothing else comes up.

8. Do you imagine because it feels right, it is right? Write down or verbally communicate your answers until nothing else comes up.

9. Does the emotion overtake you? Write down or verbally communicate your answers until nothing else comes up.

10. When your mother was emotional, how did your father react? Write down or verbally communicate your answers until nothing else comes up.

11. When your mother was emotional, how did you react? Write down or verbally communicate your answers until nothing else comes up.

12. Does your husband react the same as your father did to your mother's emotional state? Write down or verbally communicate your answers until nothing else comes up.

CONCLUSION

Emotions need to be acknowledged, you need to be aware of how you feel. It rarely helps to increase intimacy in relationship when you try to use thoughts to handle your emotions. So, to have a complete relationship, you have to 1) acknowledge your emotional state; and 2)) ask yourself, Where does this emotional state come from? Do your emotional states come from your parents and how they interrelated with one another? For example, for men, if your father dissociated when your mother got emotional, you will probably do the same thing. For women with dissociative fathers, you will probably pick someone who doesn't understand, experience, or appreciate your feelings.

In conclusion, to have a more *intimate relationship* we need to learn how to expand our awareness of our own and our partner's level of reality. One of the reasons emotional relationships lose intimacy and closeness is because we try to dominate one level of reality with another. This can be the substitution of thoughts for feelings or vice-versa. But since emotions are so strong and certainly less under our control, than thoughts, it is important to see the emotional point of view since it is so powerful. So, to have a more *intimate relationship*, you have to be able to validate your feelings and those of your partner, to see them as part of the mosaic or the tapestry of the relationship. It is not the only part of the tapestry but it is an essential part. Relationships, like a tapestry, start to unravel when one part of the tapestry is pulled on while everything else is ignored, especially the bigger picture, which is the relationship itself. It's a little like not seeing the forest for the trees. Not only do you neglect the tapestry for one particular piece of the material, but often you are unaware that you yourself are focusing on one thread (level) rather than the entire picture (all the dimensions).

TEN

THE BIOLOGY OF RELATIONSHIPS

Probably the most confused aspect of all relationships is the biological dimension. As Freud pointed out more than one hundred years ago, sexuality is so repressed and so sublimated (substituted) that it is nearly impossible for people to be in touch with what is really going on biologically. What we have to understand in this is that, on a biological level, we are talking about a sensual, sexual, and, in a word, bio-chemical resonance.

Long-term intimate sexuality is not really about mechanics, i.e., I like the way you do this, you like the way I do that, etc. There is a deeper, more organic level, namely, the *bio-chemistry*, which precedes and moves faster than the thinking, psychological, or emotional dimensions and which involves smell and taste. Noted Fourth Way master, G. I. Gurdjieff has said that, "Sensations move much faster than thought or emotion." And Alfred Korzybski, the father of General Semantics, proved as early as the 1930s that for the brain and nervous system, sensation is much closer to the quantum level or underlying unity than thoughts or even emotions. Hence, *sensation and biochemistry is closer to what is.*

So you need to ask yourself, Do you **crave** the person? Do you love how they **smell**? Do you love how they **taste**? If you do not crave their smell and taste, you won't want to be affectionate. If you do not crave a person, then you are not going to want to be sensual, sexual, or affectionate. All too often clients have complained to me that their partners aren't affectionate. But you cannot make someone be affectionate, sensual, or sexual. *They have to want to*, of their own accord; in other words, *it must come from within them.* They must **crave** you.

So the biochemical relates to our basic biology, a level uncontrollable and very real, and for many, outside of their awareness. And since it is outside of awareness, it is pre-verbal, pre-imagistic, and hard-wired into the nervous system. It is organic, part of their body itself. For instance, do you like vanilla, chocolate, or pistachio? Maybe strawberry? Well, you didn't decide this, not consciously anyway.

The reason for problems in relationships is that these levels on the relationship map get confused. In other words, often people like each other on an external or a thinking level, but they do not resonate biologically. Or you like talking with someone and share similar values but do not actually like doing the same things externally. Or—and this is a frequent complaint—you enjoy their friendship and get along psychologically, but there is no biological resonance. Or conversely, you resonate on a biological level but not on a thinking, emotional or external level.

What must be understood is that *biochemistry* is not under our conscious control but hard-wired into our nervous system. Or, in the words of the famous song of the 1970s, "When you're hot, you're hot—and when you're not, you're not." In other words, the *biochemical relationship* cannot actually be directly worked on. It is more important to realize that we have a hunger for the smell and taste of another rather than trying to change it. Problems arise because we try to overcome a lack of biological resonance by working from a psychological, emotional or external level. On the other hand, because the *biochemical dimension* is so powerful, we think it can override problems that exist on the other dimensions. This does not work, and this is yet another major reason for the lack of intimacy in relationships.

•••••••••••••••

THE BIOLOGY OF RELATIONSHIPS
by
Carol Agneessens, M.S.

When I hear the word *biology*, memories surface from hours spent in under-graduate science labs. I see long rows of tables lined with test-tubes, microscopes, and petri dishes with strangely colored organisms. Biology is the science of life in all its manifestations. It is an area of study concerned with living organisms—their form and structure, behavior and function, origin and development. The science of biology seems a distant cousin to intimate human relationship, yet the very nature of organic entwining reflects biology, which lies at the core of our living, breathing, physical selves. And, as I will illustrate in the following pages, this essential part of our nature is too often a neglected and overlooked aspect of relationship.

There seem to be myriad compensations used to replace or change our essential biological needs and drives. They may work for a time; but eventually they are subsumed into twists and repressions which are later relegated to the psychological domain. As Reich would say, our repression of biological drives often results in further psychological abstractions, denials, and distancing from our humanness. Our biology—the most neglected facet of intimate relationship—is thus the essential ground and sustaining glue for deepening and furthering intimacy.

In this context, the biology of relationship refers to the physical, chemical, and very palpable dimensions of interaction—body to body, skin to skin, flesh to flesh. Behind that first arousing glimpse of a potential *other* lies a bubbling cauldron of biochemicals coursing through the fluid systems of the physical body. Smells, textures, tastes, and fantasies arise from this neurochemical brew spurring on the dance of attraction. When clients talk about their sexuality, most reveal that although they were attracted to their partner in the beginning stages, they have since lost interest in the physical aspects of interaction. For many couples, the tensional charge of sexual attraction neutralizes over time. The ease, security and comfort accompanying long-term partnering, often causes sexual desire to diminish. Over time, partners become like a brother or sister, easy to be around, comfortable, fun—Platonic and non-sexual.

Often this state of familial co-habiting is accepted as a natural progression with age or years together. Some people say that it is a welcome respite from the no longer enjoyable sensuality of intimacy. "We don't do it anymore," is a common refrain among these clients. As comfortable as an asexual relationship may appear, it is important to recognize that this condition relegates both body and biology to their repressed religious and historical roots: that which is tolerated rather than lived in and through. How much more crucial to allow the revitalizing energy of the body's unique sensuality to explode the dimensions of relationship in such a way that experience is deepened from within and also with one's partner.

I've been using the words *sexuality* and *sensuality* interchangeable, but they really describe two very different qualities. Sensuality arises through the senses and their organic connection to elemental forces. The aroma of body, the fragrance of rain-washed hair, the aliveness radiating from within another human being are some examples. Or perhaps, the earth on my feet, the small, soft rain on my face, the smell of night-blooming jasmine from the garden. No matter what the specifics, each is another aspect of feeling a connection to physicalness to what is natural. The fecundity, the bounteous pleasure, the poignant and expectant spring in budding flowers— these are all aspects of our physicalness.

But unfortunately, for cultural, religious, societal, and individual reasons, our bodies are often considered more as functional machines than as living, sensing wholes. Sensuality thus expresses the senses when they are unconfined by the judging and restricting reigns of the intellect. We cannot feel with our heads, yet it is in our heads that we attempt to feel. Allowing awareness through opening sensory channels rather than cortical pathways ignites natural body intelligence. Most people have diminished or closed down body sensation, body knowing, and aliveness. Trusting carnal intelligence has been replaced by relying on information that can be calibrated and proven. Sensory knowing, expressed as a sensation from our belly, is often restricted the moment it arises. Trusting *gut* level intelligence, emerging to an openness about sensory stimulation and sensation—these are what we seem so ready to give up. But to learn how to once again feel and know, through the grounded base of body, revitalizes the lost instinctual self, our animal heritage.

So many of the people I see come to Rolfing and movement to reclaim sensation. Initially, many clients complain they cannot feel. What I discover is that much of their body is numb. When asked to describe the part of their body where they feel most of their energy they say their head or some place from their neck up, or behind their eyes. I will often ask clients during the intake interview, What they experience on a physical level. They often say that they do not have a sense of even sitting in the chair, or where their feet are located. As we begin our sessions together, I continue to ask for their self-awareness beneath my hands or to locate their foot, heel, or leg in relation to the space I am touching. Together we begin to reclaim the lost sense of body and the forgotten sensuous self.

The body is sensuous and spacious—it is delicious, luscious, and juicy, words describing the pleasure of eating mangoes, and also the joy of being and feeling the body from inside out. But again, for many people, sensation is not enjoyable, but something to be controlled or even feared. The minute they feel any type of sensuality or body feeling, they immediately dampen the experience, or abstract into a label (this sensation is sad, angry, or fearful). Or they will make up some kind of a story which is immediately linked with the particular sensation. Often sensation is interpreted as sexual. Sensation is sensation and is the ground for body aliveness which is inherently sensual. Sensations may be sexual, but they do not have to be, or if they are sexual, they don't have to be acted on. Unfortunately, limiting body sense over the years and even over the centuries, has relegated physical sensation to the realm of something sexual which consequently needs to be controlled. If we want to move forward on the path toward reclaiming our physical minds (i.e., our body knowing), it is necessary to experience sensation as a positive, vitalizing force, and to allow it to be, without label, judgment or story.

Belief systems about sensuality, the body, etc., are often part of the repressive mechanism keeping individuals from their physicalness. Part of the challenge is to get clear about what our belief systems are concerning our own body and then work from there. When we accept sensations, we support the emergence of sensual wholeness.

BODY DIALOGUE: WHERE ARE YOU AWARE

Sitting comfortably, notice your breath. Now, pay attention to the parts of your body which you feel (i.e. our head, a pain, your back etc.) Do not try to change anything; just be aware. What comes to mind when you say *sensuous*? Does your body constrict, do you relax, does your breathing change? What images come to mind when you imagine something *sensuous*? Where in your body do you pull away from feeling sensuous, where do you move toward sensation? Notice what parts of your body you become aware in relation to feeling sensuous.

BODY DIALOGUE: FUSIONS

Take the information from the above exercise and notice what the word *sensuous* is fused with. For example let's imagine that when you ask what sensuality is fused with, the word *shame* pops up.

1) If you fuse sensuous with shame what gets created? Sinful desiring? Is there anywhere in this present time body that you feel sinful and desiring. Take the label off and experience it as energy.

2) If you fuse sensuous with shame what doesn't get created? Freedom? What did you assume, decide or believe that got you to not create freedom? Where in this present time body did you not create freedom.

3) If you fuse sensuality and shame what is resisted? It is resisting sexual expression. Where in this present time body to you experience resisting sexual expression. Take the label off and return it to a state of energy.

4) If you separate sensuality and shame what is your experience?

5) If you separate sensuality and shame what does not occur?

Express an idea you have about sensuality and 'shame. Tell me another idea. Tell me another idea.

France is one of the few countries in the Western world where sensuality is admired and valued. The French openly celebrate their sensuality. You can see this in the way people dress, the way men and women look at each other, and in their love of good food, wine, and pleasure. Size, age and shape do not dominate a woman's expression of her beauty as they do in the US. All of this does not mean that people act out their every impulse; but that there is an inherent permission to enjoy the beauty of the body and of living in general.

One of my goals in working is to faciliate an individual's reclaiming of their body feeling and sensation, even though many people express a revulsion about their body. I see lack of feeling and body hatred as having similar roots—roots which went unnourished and were not sturdy enough to support any kind of robust health and life. Though these roots reach back into childhood and may even be generational legacies they can still be regenerated so that individuals can experience full body responsiveness and contact in their relationships.

BODY DIALOGUE: MAPPING JUDGMENT

Sitting comfortably, notice the weight of your body on the chair or floor. What are you aware of in your body? Imagine a three-dimensional map of your body. Notice the width, depth and length of your body map. Can you fill in more of the details, or is your body map too one dimensional, peopled with stick figures? Ask yourself which parts of your body-map reveal areas of judgment or unacceptance. Let those spaces light up, do not change anything. For right now, all I ask is for you to just notice things.

CYCLES OF DESIRE

Cycles of waning and waxing desire are organic rhythms, and are as natural as those observed in the midnight sky, or in the phases of moon, all of which reflect cycles of coming and going. It is as inconceivable to desire someone all the time as it is for the tides to remain high. The ebb and flow fluctuate, yet the connection, the flowing between partners, is always there. Desiring your partner, their smell, their taste, and their touch are natural expressions of a biological craving for them. I'm not talking about missing them or going to the movies with someone you like being with. Craving is biologically based. Craving rests somewhere on the edge of hunger. It is as if, without their touch and their embrace you might starve. The biological aspects of relationship are real, yet they are often obscured by our mental images of who we think would make a perfect match, or because we are lonely for a companion. When the biological dimension is ignored, trouble often arises later in the relationship.

The glue of relationships is physical, sexual/sensual pleasuring, loving each other, touching each other. Smell, shape and size all matter between partners. A deep and pleasurable body connection at the beginning of a relationship often sustains relationship during difficult times. It is important to look toward the other for a softening of the edges created by an often harsh and senseless world. Early in our relationship, my partner and I made an agreement, if we are engaged in a heated argument, we will always get out of bed first. Our bed is where we experience pleasure whether from a good night's rest or from our mutual nuzzling and loving each other.

YIELDING INTO ANOTHER

The neurological pattern of yielding, of resting into another not inertly but with contact, is also a way of finding the sensation of support and stability. If you have ever seen a baby, you understand the radiant peace of an infant melded into mother's arms and body. It is this quality of support in contact that allows energy to flow between lovers. I am not talking about an inert draping, but rather, an active movement. Learning to yield into your own body and then with your partner opens the gateway for satisfying physical and energetic exchange.

EXPLORING YIELD

Lie on your belly in a very comfortable space. Allow your-self to let your belly go into the support of the floor, ground, or surface you are contacting. If you imagine your belly button to be a small stone allow it to fall toward the center of the earth. Notice how your body eases and rests when yield becomes an action. From yield all other actions are possible: we can push, reach toward. Yield is contactful and support-ive. And is essential to deepening intimacy at a biological level.

ELEVEN

THE HEART:
THE ESSENTIAL DIMENSION

The **HEART**: **THE ESSENTIAL CONNECTION** can best be summarized as a resonance which is experienced being to being. **THE HEART IS ESSENTIAL** and is prior to your taste, your smell, and your vision. The **inner spaciousness** of your **ESSENCE AND THE HEART** is prior to all of your conditioning. When we meet somebody, and feel that *heart* energy, that is when we are experiencing our **ESSENCE**. This pure experience without filters is an energetic **HEART-TO-HEART**, or **ESSENCE-to-ESSENCE** relationship. Of course, you can be in **ESSENCE** without having a partner or a relationship. But since we are talking about relationships, we all know the fabulous feeling to be in the **ESSENCE** of **HEART** with another in an *intimate relationship*.

The problem which can emerge is you have an **ESSENCE** or a deep **HEART** resonance with someone; but absolutely nothing on a psychological or emotional level. Perhaps if the **HEART-TO-HEART** resonance is strong enough then you begin to interpret that it means more or something else other than an **ESSENCE** to **ESSENCE HEART RESONANCE**. Often times, there might be an **essential** resonance and you imagine that this means an upcoming sexual intensity when there isn't. What you can begin to see is that all of these different experiences and levels of relating have a particular and different function. And it is difficult to override or substitute one level of relating with another. Again, I know many people who meet somebody, have a very deep **HEART RESONANCE**, but their relationships don't work and lack intimacy. Why? Because they keep on fantasizing that the heart is enough. The heart isn't enough. Actually no *one* level is enough to sustain intimacy. It is an interrelationship of levels of relating which provides more *intimate relationships*. Simply put, *the greater the number of relationship levels available, the more whole and complete is an intimate relationship. The fewer of the relationship levels available, the less whole or complete is an intimate relationship.*

The greater the number of dimensions that two people can resonate on, the higher the probability of a successful relationship. You need to be in sync on other levels to have a successful relationship. The *heart* and the *bio-chemical resonance* are usually what lures us into a relationship. The problem is that no matter how deep a *heart* or *bio-chemical resonance*, it doesn't mean you will share the same values (thinking level), feel the same about things and be able to communicate (emotional dimension), and it certainly doesn't mean that you will enjoy doing the same things (external dimension). Appreciating this allows us look at the *heart resonance*, being to being, and to notice that if you try to override, overcome, or substitute one level of relationship for another level, it generally yields pain..

ESSENCE is truly the **HEART** of the matter since **ESSENCE** is where your **HEART** is. Often, you can have an incredible resonance with somebody on a *heart* level, but no resonance with them sexually or in the external world. It's one of the strangest things that happens between people, a really mysterious phenomena. I recall maybe walking into a market and having this unbelievable *heart resonance* with the woman standing behind the counter. At the same time, when I get up there and talk with her, there is nothing to say, nothing to communicate, no common ground of shared experience between us. It doesn't mean that she's bad or good, all it means is that we have an **ESSENCE-to-ESSENCE HEART RESONANCE** but we do not have a relationship on any other level.

Love Fusions

Love is such a potent experience and so intrinsic to our being that a lack of it can cause a fusion between love and some kind of action. For example, love can be fused with money, and another hot button area (no pun intended) fused with sex.

The Love Process

Rarely is love for love's sake experienced. Love is generally fused or associated with action, feeling, thoughts, etc. Since your ideas about a thing is not the thing, all your ideas about love are not love and must be acknowledged and discarded. In this way, you can have the Essential Quality of love which is love for love's sake or love with no object.

EXERCISE

Pair up with your partner or potential partner. The purpose of this exercise is to notice and sort out your love fusions so you can have love for love's sake.

Part I:

Facing your partner, Start off sentences with; and fill in the blank:

1) If I take in your love, I might feel <u>(fill in the blank)</u>.

For example, if I take in your love, "<u>Then I will feel obligated</u>." If I take in your love, "<u>Then I feel like I have to reciprocate</u>." If I take in your love, "<u>Then I feel I'm being engulfed</u>," or "<u>I have to withdraw or there'll be no me</u>," etc.

Keep repeating the question until nothing more emerges. (Notice what pops up and discard it.)

Part II:

Pair up with your partner. Start off a sentence with: "If I feel love, then I have to <u>(fill in the blank)</u>."

For example, If I feel love then I have to "Go along with what you say or do." If I feel love, "Then it means "<u>I have to hug you</u>." If I feel love, then it means "<u>I have to make dinner for you</u>," etc. Keep repeating the question until nothing more emerges. (Notice what pops up and discard it.)

Love is a highly charged issue. It is important to love for love's sake, without it being asssociated to anything else, or with a "so that <u>(fill in the blank)</u>. Cutting this associational "love" loop is imperative to stabilize this quality and all Essential qualities (see *Way of the Human*, Volume III).

EXERCISE: DEFINE LOVE

For each definition answer the following questions verbally or writing it down with your partner or potential partner.

1) Define love.
2) Regarding that definition, what assumptions have I made?
3) What have been the consequences of those assumptions?
4) Am I still making those assumptions today?
5) What beliefs have I created around this concept of love?
6) What have been the consequences of those beliefs?
7) Am I still believing those today?
8) What decisions have I made?
9) What have been the consequences of those decisions?
10) Am I still deciding that today?
    Examples of these are:
    Love equals being needed
    Love equals feeling safe
    Love equals feeling trapped
    Love equals being the only one in your life

CONCLUSION

What is pivotal in relationship is acknowleding where you do or do not relate in your *intimate relationships*, honestly, without judgment, evaluation, significance, blame, shame, labeling or diagnosing self or other, or allowing the change mechanism to take over. Then, determining where, if anywhere you proceed on the intimacy or relationship continuum.

Experiential Conclusion

1) Without using your thoughts, emotions, memory, associations or perceptions, is there no-love, love or neither?

2) Without using your thoughts, emotions, memory, associations or perceptions are you lovable, unlovable or neither.

3) Without using your thoughts, emotions, memory, associations or perceptions, what is love?

TWELVE

THE SPIRITUAL DIMENSION

Quantum Psychology defines spirituality as an awareness of the underlying unity which joins us all. Now, of course, in a relationship with another person, it is not so much that you are aware of the underlying unity, but that you understand that there is a spiritual level to relationship. This is the *understanding* that there is something greater than your individual personality. This doesn't necessarily mean that you are in touch with the underlying unity all the time, but that you acknowledge and appreciate that something greater than you interconnects us all. You could call this underlying relationship to this consciousness, God, intelligence, it doesn't matter. What is important is that this sense of something greater be shared within the context of the relationship. For some, couples being on a spiritual path can enhance their relationship. **(HOWEVER, BEWARE, I HAVE OFTEN-TIMES SEEN PEOPLE WHO CONFUSE AND TRY UNSUCCESSFULLY TO OVERRIDE OTHER LEVELS, PARTICULARLY THE BIOLOGICAL-SEXUAL LEVEL WITH THE SPIRITUAL LEVEL.)** This doesn't mean that both partners are on the same spiritual path, or that they follow the same methods, techniques, or guru. There are many spiritual paths but the fundamental core is to develop our understanding of spirituality, and open us so that we are willing to spend some time focusing on the underlying unity.

As I said, it doesn't matter if one partner is into meditation and the other partner is into prayer. Or if one partner is into taking apart identities and another partner is into worshiping the Goddess. What does matter is recognizing the fact that there is an underlying unity regardless of method. For example, I knew a couple where the wife was into Buddhism and the husband was into Sufism and believe it or not, they had problems about it. So often in relationships, people get so identified with the techniques they are using without understanding that the goal is to be in touch with the underlying unity, which joins all of us rather than some kind of exclusionary practice in which one is right and the other wrong.

What can enhance and make a relationship wonderful is that both partners have an understanding that there is something beyond personalities, something beyond relationships, something beyond sensations, something beyond psychology, something beyond the external or biochemical connection. In view of this, techniques are relatively unimportant. What is important is that at some level there is an understanding that moving through us is an underlying unity, an underlying something, and that too is, and can be, part of our relationship.

By being aware of this underlying unity, we can see that each partner has a relationship to the "other" which is beyond their personal selves.

SUBSTITUTING THE SPIRITUAL FOR THE SEXUAL OR OTHER DIMENSIONS

I have met many couples, especially in India, who had a very deep spiritual resonance. They appreciated the same spirituality and religion, they even liked the same meditations, spiritual rituals, and discussions. But they had no sexual relationship. What kept them together temporarily was their belief structure that if they had a strong spiritual relationship, then everything else would fall into place. But still, I have never seen an intimate marriage or relationship based solely on a spiritual resonance. This substituting tendency not only exists in India—but also in our Western culture.

Recently, I met a woman from New Orleans that whenever a financial problem arose in her relationship (external), because her husband did not work and provide money for her family, she immediately tried to overcome levels for his poor treatment of her and the family (external dimension) by dissociating and spiritualizing; (substituting the spiritual dimension for the external dimension). She would even say, "He treats me like a goddess (spiritual)," or "He really knows how to treat women."

In this way, she misused spirituality and the spritual dimension to overcome their external issues. Why did she do this? It seemed that she would age-regress, and so want to merge with him that she called this age-regressed pre-the realization of separation merger, spiritual and good treatment in a feeble attempt to over-come their external problems. Unfortunately, in this subtle way, the spiritual level too can be misused to try to overcome the external or any level for that matter.

FOR THE SPIRITUAL DIMENSION— QUESTIONNAIRE

(To be done with a partner or potential partner)

1. How important is spirituality to you?

2. Do you prefer a ritualized spirituality where you go to church on a particular day?

3. Would you rather have a spirituality that is more spontaneous?

4. When taking a vacation, does part of it involve spirituality?

5. In your relationship do you try to use spirituality to overcome a poor sexual relationship or not having sex.

6. In your relationship do you try to use spirituality to overcome your thoughts?

7. In your relationship do you try to use spirituality to overcome your feelings?

8. In your relationship do you try to use spirituality to overcome your external world?

CONCLUSION

The spiritual dimension is the most neglected of all the dimensions. If the spiritual dimension is taken in along with all the other dimensions, it can make it easier for the other dimensions to expand, express themselves, and manifest their unique presence. But the spiritual dimension should not be confused with whether you're a Catholic, a Jew, a Muslim, a Sufi, a Protestant, a Hundu, Taoist or a Buddhist. What needs to be understood is that the spiritual dimension is a way of relating to the underlying unity no matter what name you call it. Normally, the path—(or *how to*)—has a tendency to be emphasized rather than the underlying unity. For that reason in your relationship, discuss and appreciate that all roads lead to Rome, and without substitution become aware of the spiritual level as a vehicle to deepen your *intimate relationships.*

THE LESS DIMENSIONS OF
MANIFESTATION WE USE AND ARE
AWARE OF, THE LOWER THE
PROBABILITY OF AN
INTIMATE RELATIONSHIP.

Stephen H. Wolinsky

RELATIONSHIPS DO NOT WORK
BECAUSE TO RESIST SEPARATION,
WE UNKNOWINGLY SACRIFICE
OURSELVES IN HOPES OF MERGER,
REMAIN IN THE PAST, AND DENY
ASPECTS OF OURSELVES, AND
HENCE, WE ALSO LOSE WHO THE
OTHER IS IN PRESENT TIME.

Stephen H. Wolinsky

AS WE EXPLORE THE DIFFERENT
DIMENSIONS OF MANIFESTATIONS,
WE WIND UP ASKING OURSELVES,
WHY DO WE CONFUSE ONE LEVEL
WITH ANOTHER? THE ANSWER IS
CLEAR: WE CONFUSE THE LEVELS
DUE TO THE SEPARATION AND
MERGER RESPONSE BY WHICH WE
SUBSTITUTE ONE LEVEL FOR
ANOTHER BECAUSE THAT IS (OR
WAS) THE ONLY LEVEL ORIGINALLY
AVAILABLE. FOR EXAMPLE,
IMAGINE A CHILD WHOSE FATHER
WAS AN ENGINEER. THE CHILD
WANTS EMOTIONAL SUPPORT, BUT
INSTEAD HE GETS AN INTELLECTUAL
CHALLENGE. OR, TAKE THE CHILD
OF AN ATHLETE WHO WANTS
INTELLECTUAL ENERGY BUT
INSTEAD GETS EXTERNAL PERKS.

IN THIS WAY INFANTS DO TWO
MAJOR THINGS. FIRST, THEY EXPECT
RE-MERGER TO OVERCOME
SEPARATION. SECOND, THEY TRY
TO RE-MERGE THROUGH A
DIMENSION OF MANIFESTATION. IF
ONE DIMENSION IS CLOSED TO
THEM, THEY TRY TO SUBSTITUTE IT
FOR ANOTHER, WITH THE EXPECTA-
TION AND GOAL OF RE-MERGING.

Stephen H. Wolinsky

THIRTEEN

SUBSTITUTION:
THE SEDUCTION OF MERGER

I'LL DO OR GIVE-UP ANYTHING
TO NOT BE SEPARATE.

The infant's expectation and re-merger fantasy, coupled with his inability to avail himself of the different avenues and vehicles of merger, causes him to substitute one level of manifestation for another. In other words, he tries to overcome the loss in one level of manifestation by using another. For example,, if the external level of merger is unavailable, then, when he grows up, he might develop a psychological-spiritual philosophy as a way to merge to justify trying to overcome one level for another. Substitution can best be defined as switching one level for another with the expectation of merger. This substituting of levels to achieve merger and resist the Realization of Separation is done because certain levels of *merger are available* while others are not.

How does this apply to relationships? When in a present time relationship there is a significant lack of potential for merger in one dimension (i.e., the biological), often there will be an attempt to overcome this deficiency through another level (the external). This expectation of re-merger—frequently experienced as, *If you were different or would change, I would merge and not feel separate, combines the change mechanism with substitution.* This occurs frequently when there is little resonance on a biological level. It is not uncommon for a couple who lack a strong physical resonance to look for other levels of merger.

THE BIOLOGICAL GLUE

To begin with, the biological is the biological ground of relationship. The desire for relationship begins biologically and is hard-wired into the nervous system as reproduction and the survival of the species. But as was said before, the biological is denied more frequently than any other dimension. Why? Because through the socialization process, from childhood on, we are continually and implicitly asked to deny biological function.

For example, not to eat when hungry, but at specific times, not to wake up when feeling rested but when it's time to go to school, there are a million others. To overcome how we feel (emotional-biological level) we work long hours at jobs (external level). Somehow in covert ways, merger (with mom), is later substituted for approval or achievement. In this way,

merger is implicitly promised through the denial of the biological and other levels. This overcoming the body is often the message which religion offers, promising *merger* with God (mom) if we deny the flesh.

SUBSTITUTING THE EXTERNAL
FOR THE BIOLOGICAL

You see many couples that try to substitute the external level for the biological as a way to experience intimacy. For example, Jane and Brad are both musicians. They initially related through their music and performance lifestyles. The excitement was created by their joint compositions and concerts; and they described playing together as joyous and deeply intimate. Jane and Brad went on to cultivate a romantic relationship even though they both admitted that the sexual part of their relationship never got off the ground. Together they decided it really didn't matter because the music they created made up for it. As time went on, Jane began to feel a lack of intimacy and a need for deeper closeness. Though they tried to develop this area of their relationship, they could never quite make it happen and both ended up very frustrated.

Both Jane and Brad struggled with their situation until in therapy they came to terms with the truth that they were better suited as friends and musical partners rather than romantic partners. Jane and Brad are both happily married today. But not to each other. Ten years later, they still perform and compose music together.

SUBSTITUTING THE BIOLOGICAL FOR THE *FILL IN THE BLANK*

Couples may divert their lack of biological passion into financial or professional achievement, raising children, social or community service, or some kind of mutual productivity. On the surface all of these seem sensible and philosophically justifiable. However, this using the external dimension to overcome a lack or deficiency in the biological dimension often-times yields problems.

Life itself may put us in situations where external events or situations divert us away from nurturing our biological intimacy. Periods such as child-rearing, career development, financial stress, aging parents, or illness may all temporarily suppress the physical relationship. Yet, a lot depends on whether the biological dimension was strong in the first place.

If the *biochemistry* was strong, and if interpersonal dynamics can be kept clear from unexpressed resentments it *might* be possible to rekindle the biological. This is best done through touch and closeness, and by creating times to be together. What we are suggesting is the importance of understanding the different dimensions and where you are with regard to your partner. It is important not to substitute but rather to feel the pain of the separation and the accompanying False Core. When you allow yourself to feel this pain, you can then begin to explore where you are with your partner as far as the dimensions are concerned, and to not substitute but communicate with each other.

We often seek to merge with our partners in whatever way is available, and substitute one dimension for another even if it is not always with the end result that we want. To illustrate, there are many couples who are constantly fighting with each other, producing strong physical and emotional responses and releases in lieu of having sex. Then there are couples who practice some form of celibacy in the name of spirituality and seldom engage in sexual or physical intimacy.

Tara and Michael came into therapy because they were going through a crisis in their relationship. Their history revealed that sexual intimacy had never part of their relationship because of their adherence to a yoga community they belonged to. They said that their daily meditation practice, which they did together every morning and evening, was more important to them. The crisis came with Michael's disclosure of a two-year affair with a woman who was not a member of the spiritual community. This brought everything to a climax (no pun intended). What had happened was that Tara and Michael had a strong relationship on the levels of the external world and in **ESSENCE**. Because of the "spiritual" joining, they had attempted to substitute the biological dimension with the spiritual dimension. As mentioned before, you can't solve the problems of one dimension by using another

dimension; such a maneuver only makes things more com-
plicated as the problems subtly continue. Or, simply stated,
*meet the problem (or dimension) at the level of the problem
(or dimension).*

IF YOU SUBSTITUTE A
PSYCHOLOGICAL OR SPIRITUAL
DIMENSION FOR THE
BIOLOGICAL, THE BIOLOGICAL
GETS SUPPRESSED. WHEN THE
BIOLOGICAL IS SUPPRESSED THE
ENERGY WILL FIND AN AVENUE OF
RELEASE THROUGH A DIFFERENT
DIMENSION.

THE PROBLEM IS, SINCE IT IS NOT
THE APPROPRIATE LEVEL AND YOU
ARE TRYING TO OVERCOME ONE
DIMENSION BY THE USE OF
ANOTHER—YOU'RE GOING TO
GET THE OVERUSE OF ONE LEVEL
TO OVERRIDE ANOTHER, FOR
EXAMPLE, OVERACHIEVEMENT
(A WORKAHOLIC RELATIONSHIP)
TO OVERCOME THE LACK OF BIO-
LOGICAL INTIMACY OR, IF THE BIO-
LOGICAL ENERGY IS TURNED
AGAINST ITSELF, YOU CAN EXPERI-
ENCE ILLNESS ON A
PHYSICAL LEVEL, OR DEPRESSION
ON AN EMOTIONAL LEVEL.

Stephen H. Wolinsky

When I lived in India, the sexual repression was over-whelming. People forced themselves to be celibate try to over-come the biological with the spiritual, which resulted in con-tinual emotional outbursts, external power struggles; and, ironically, over-thinking even though meditation was sup-posed to get you to go beyond thought. Furthermore, all of this that went on in the name of spirituality was actually the result of mis-information about biology.

Hugh and Diana came to therapy and reported that they experienced instant rapport and heartfelt connection when they first met each other through common friends. Diana was re-covering from a fifteen year marriage in the Mormon reli-gion and had five children. With her divorce two years earlier and subsequent excommunication from her church, Diana struggled to stay involved with her children. There were many conflicts and battles with her ex-husband. Her children were angry at her for leaving the marriage and their religion. The children refused to be in her life if she dated or saw any po-tential new partners. All this created tension for Diana and Hugh in their attempts to create a relationship. Eventually the conflict became so great, Diana decided to terminate the relationship with Hugh until she could find an easier way to see her children while rebuilding her own life.

This last case is an example of how a couple may have a very strong resonance at the level of **ESSENCE**, and yet on the external level, through no fault of their own, lacked com-patibility. Many couples will painfully struggle to try to make their relationship work because their resonance at the level of **ESSENCE** is so rich and meaningful, even with lifestyle differences that prohibit the development of a more well-rounded relationship which includes other dimensions. Such difficulties as long-distance relationships, lifestyle choices, children, and religion may all contribute to external condi-tions that cannot support the relationship, even if the reso-nance in the *heartfelt* love of **ESSENCE** is deep.

If we go through the dimensions, we can see that there may be one dimension that is the particular glue of the relationship, the one that the couple depend on in order to compensate for lack on another level.

Sharon and George were both professors at a university. They surrounded themselves with a rich intellectual community and prided themselves in their commitments to keep the relationship alive with intellectual and political pursuits. They thrived on their discussions and the communication between them was rich and complex. They felt they truly understood each other. But their relationship lacked an emotional dimension. Whenever Sharon wanted to express her deeper emotional responses to George, they had problems. George would shut down and point out her lack of reasonable thinking. Over time, Sharon became more dissociated from her feelings, finding no avenue for them in her relationship with George. In order to keep the marriage alive, she was forced to abandon her own needs for emotional closeness, and relate with George solely on the thinking dimension.

CONCLUSION

It can be valuable to look at our *intimate relationships* to see if one dimension is being over-used or over-emphasized in the place of another. It is also important to see if we are focusing on one dimension in order to avoid separation or to over-compensate for a lack in another dimension. Then, the question to be asked is, If this is so, what effect does this have for me individually and for us as a couple?

FOURTEEN

SELF LIES: I MUST AVOID SEPARATION

What causes self-lies? The resistance to separation. What causes *expectations* of merger. Self lies. The entire process is a vicious cycle: Separation → expectation of merger, → self lies → greater *expectations* → the change mechanism → frustration → substitution → frustration, → self lies → separation, etc.

How often have we been involved with someone and discovered quite unexpectedly that they had qualities, behaviors, or desires we hadn't previously realized they had. We are taken aback, maybe even feel betrayed. "How could this have happened?" we wonder, "How did I miss this?" It's like the old cliché that love is blind, especially in the early stages of a relationship where we want to see the other in the most desirable light, especially if there is a strong physical and emotional attraction. We want the "we" to happen so badly that we may lie to ourselves albeit unknowingly. When this happens, we may miss certain indicators, or block them out and deny them altogether from entering into our awareness.

One client entered therapy because she was astonished and disturbed upon realizing that her boyfriend was not going to give up his partying lifestyle. She had rationalized that his behavior would change once he was in a committed relationship. Reality hit hard after five months of dating and he was still spending a substantial amount time going to bars. She finally ran out of excuses to herself and had to face the bitter truth. The questions that were asked were, "What lies did you tell yourself in relation to your boyfriend? What lies did you tell yourself in order to overlook what he was really like?" What emerged was her underlying fear. "I don't want to be separate."

If it is true, as some have said, that all you need to know about a person is revealed within the early part of a relationship, then why don't we see it? It's because we don't want to be separate. Our fear of separation is so powerful that we *lie* to ourelves and then *lie* that we lied.

Lewis and Cynthia met in a singles bar. Lewis was slightly drunk and was a bartender, Cynthia was a real estate broker. They decided to meet for dinner on Friday at 7:00. Cynthia arrived waiting on time but Lewis was an hour late and clearly had been drinking. Cynthia lied to herself and thought, "Oh, he's not this way, things will be different later." Two years passed, and Cynthia complained to me in an angry and surprised manner, "He's always drinking and always comes late. I'm really angry that he's like this. But no matter how much we talk, he never changes how he acts." Once again I confronted her with the question, "What *lies* have you told yourself regarding Lewis?" At first, she got huffy; but later confessed the *lies* she told herself about his drinking and lateness even on their *first* date.

CONCLUSION
Self Lies and Substitution

Self lies promise you happiness, but only create more problems. But it is important to realize that we don't *lie* to ourselves because we are bad or sneaky. We *lie* to ourselves because the fear of separation and our resistance to re-experiencing the wound can be so powerful. It is sometimes the only way our nervous system knows how to overcome it and survive. But we need to realize that our survival mechanism is hard-wired into our nervous system; it is not something that we consciously produce. The nervous system does not want the pain of the shock of the Realization of Separation to ever happen again.

From this longing for merger, self-lies and substitutions arise. Once we realize what our self-lies are and how they damage our relationships, we will see that they don't protect us from the pain of separation, but only prolong the long dull ache with depression and over-compensating to avoid separation. By seeing what our self-lies are, we can stop blaming the other with the change mechanism, substituting, and take responsiblility for the *lies* we told ourselves which got us in the relationship problems we are experiencing. With this level of personal responsibility, acceptance can often becomes possible.

ONCE YOU CAN SEE THE OTHER IN
PRESENT TIME AS A HUMAN BEING,
EXPECTATIONS DIMINISH AND THE
ESSENTIAL QUALITY OF
ACCEPTANCE INCREASES.

ACCEPTANCE IS NOT A
PSYCHOLOGICAL QUALITY.
ACCEPTANCE IS AN ESSENTIAL
QUALITY WHICH ARISES WHEN
YOUR AND THE OTHER'S
HUMANNESS IS REALIZED. ONCE
THIS OCCURS YOU HAVE ACCEP-
TANCE WHICH IS LOVE.

Stephen H. Wolinsky

FIFTEEN

TRANCES RELATIONSHIP S LIVE: THE SEPARATION BUFFER

TRANCES, TRANCES AND MORE TRANCES

In my first book, *Trances People Live* (1990), I defined trance in two ways: First, trance is a shrinking of the focus of attention; and second, trance occurs through a series of inter-actions designed to create an altered state of consciousness.

To illustrate the first definition, in relationships, people shrink their focus of attention, omitting much input from the external world and selecting out only a small fraction. This is done with the desire to merge or to resist separation.

In the second definition, the series of interactions occurs self-to-self in order to convince oneself that what is, is not what is, as a way to avoid separation and merge. It illustrate how they both work hand-in-hand, let us look at the origin of denial. In denial, a series of interactions occurs between the self and other to avoid separation or in hopes of merger. For example, the man who has no money or work potential in-duces a trance in his partner that success and money are as-sured. The partner to avoid separation in the hopes of merger, shrinks her focus of attention, omits (lies), selects-out, and believes him, even in the face of contradictory evidence, such as no money, work, angry outbursts, etc. *It does take two to tango, and two to go into a relationship trance.*

To break the relationship trance, the resistance to separation and desiring merger must be experienced and processed, and the lies and substituting of levels confronted.

Below are some of the multitudes of possible relationship trances:

The Different Trance

One of the great buffers to the pain of separation and resistance to separation is the **Different Trance**. The different trance begins as all other relationship trances: I feel separation, I feel pain and to reduce the pain I go into the **different trance**. In this trance, I believe that things are *different*, or you are not or are different than who you present yourself to be. What governs this different trance? The wish to overcome separation and re-merge. It is for this reason that we use trances to buffer against separation.

The Addition Trance

In **Addition Trance**, we add meaning to something our partner said or did in order to fit our fantasy or wish. This fuels the expectation of merger. We may end up creating a whole movie in our heads about who this person is which may have absolutely no bearing on reality. Then, we go on acting as if that picture were true. Later on, dis-illusionment sets in. (We do not see *dis-illusionment* as negative—rather, it means the end of illusions and facing reality.) Yet seldom do we take personal responsibility for our own *illusionment*. Rather, when the person does not match or meet our often implicit merger requirements, it is easier to blame them and feel incredibly hurt.

The "We can work it out" Trance

The next common relationship trance (which, of course, re-enforces the system, is, *We can work it out*. I was trained in family therapy for more than three years; and I used to jokingly say that I had on my business cards WE CAN WORK IT OUT. This Let's Work It Out—why this? why that?—generally begs the question of, I feel separate because you did not merge with me. Later, this is reframed and rather than saying, "You do not merge with me," you say, "You did not meet me," or "I want someone to meet me."

When this meeting-merger does not take place, people in their unconscious desire for merger oftentimes become the other's reflection and give themselves up to the other in hopes of merger. In this way, to avoid the pain of separation, we give up our priorities. We now take a back-seat and "act out" the expectation merger fantasy, which often results in feelings of resentment and deprivation. We may forfeit something we like, no longer expressing our own opinions because they oppose our partner's, or even deny or become unaware of our needs or even that we have needs. Anything to avoid separation and stay with them in what is a merger fantasy.

Hypervigilant Trance

Clients of mine have developed what I call the **Hypervigilant Trance** whereby the adult age-regresses and tries to *mind-read* what they imagine the "other" wants. Then they try to match (merge) with the other by giving them their fantasized response, so as not to feel separate.

I was once told by a therapist a story of a client who, to avoid separation, would go on high-risk backpacking adventures with an older man she wanted to connect with. On the surface she presented that she was interested in such extreme activities, yet she really lied to herself and to him as well, and she lied so that he would want to be with her and she would not feel separate. Later on she came to terms that they really didn't match in this area. Perhaps she thought he would not want to date her unless she shared his level of adventure. This giving-up of oneself to resist separation in hopes of merger, is what has now been called in our common vernacular *co-dependency*.

The Love Is Blind Trance

Characteristics or behaviors which show up in the beginning of a relationship may not have the same impact or significance further into the relationship. The **Love is Blind trance** disguises our own reactions so that we may fail to acknowledge a demon which might later rear its head. An example of this would be a person who goes blind to the fact that the person they were dating had no money. Initially they might lie to themselves about this, but later find they become resentful and critical of their partner for this very trait.

The Compartmentalized Trance

One man came in for therapy describing how he loved the woman he was seeing but he was concerned about how she treated her children. He thought she was over-controlling and too dominating. At the same time, he was quick to defend her because it was difficult for him to express his feelings about the situation. To avoid separation, he went into the **Compartmentalized Trance**. He told himself that he would have a relationship only with her and stay away from her when she was with her children. He refused to engage in family activities, and deceived himself into believing it wouldn't matter. I have also seen many people who pretended not to notice how their partners expressed their destructive anger. They minimized what would later would be the single most harmful component to their relationship. All to avoid separation.

The "It Could be Worse Trance"

This trance is, "Well, I can't leave because it could be worse." I had a client once who, after twenty years of marriage, said, "The last fifteen years was bad, the sex was obligatory." I asked her why she stayed on, and she said, "Well, if I find someone else, I'll just repeat the pattern, and most people I know who leave relationships wind up *trading-down*." This is how she justified her resistance to separation, and normalizing pain, i.e., this is how relationships are—in other words, the **It Could Be Worse Trance**.

In this latter trance, the person does not realize they are age-regressing and duplicating parental patterns. In this way, pain is normalized in order to avoid separation. In these scenarios, oftentimes the change mechanism kicks in, i.e., if he would only change— everything would be fine. Thus, she focuses on the "other" and avoids her own age-regressed separation issues.

The Change Trance

Many times we operate under the assumption that the other person will change, or that our love will heal or bring out the best in the other. This **Change Trance** is rooted in our infantile belief that by changing mom, later generalized to the "other," the separation pain will disappear. It can further be compounded with the **love trance** of, *My love will change them*. These beliefs are based on the premise that through love, mom will change or they will change, and we will be able to merge with them. This self deception is based on our failure to accept the separation dilemma. When we refuse to deal with the separation pain, we allow ourselves to slip into this trance, and no longer see the other person for who they are. It is as if we could magically change everything simply because we want to or because of our love.

The Potential Trance

Another possible pitfall, the **Potential Trance**, occurs when we fall in love with the potential we see in our partner. We have glimpses of a *potentially* nurturing person, a *potentially* successful person, a *potentially* emotionally healthy person, etc. etc. They appear to us as diamonds in the rough which our love can help reveal. At some point, we believe in their *potential* more than in the reality of who they presently are.

Unfortunately, in many situations a person stays in an unsatisfactory relationship waiting for their partner's potential to manifest. Self-deception causes them to deny the truth of the situation and the personality of their partners. It's like the title of one of the first publications on co-dependency for women by Robin Norwood, Women Who Love too Much: When You Keep Wishing and Hoping They'll Change.

One of the best ways to break through this trance is to ask yourself, "Am I happy with who my partner is now? Not someday when they make more money, lose weight, go to school, stop drinking, etc." *What you see is what you get.* Assume they are not going to change. Ever. Is that enough for you to stay with this person?

Frequently, when clients tell me that they really saw the other's *potential,* I am reminded of the sculptor, Pygmalion. In this myth, he carved out the image of his beloved and, like Narcissus, fell in love with his own creation, his own reflection. We see who we fantasize our partner could be versus who they are. Perhaps we feel that the transformative power of love or the relationship itself will do the trick. Perhaps we believe that the annoying behavior, which reminds us that we are separate, will change in the course of our being together since love conquers all—or so we believe.

One woman I worked with fell in love with a man who showed no personal ambition. She said she was upset about his lack of worldly success. She pumped him up and got him to believe in himself enough to return to school and get a master's degree. But after finishing his training, he decided he was not cut out for the role and returned to his on-again/off-again work habits. What had happened was that in the *potential trance* she had seen his *potential* in this man which was not there. Why? To avoid separation. She lied to herself and believed her own lies that her dreams of success could be fulfilled with him. He then merged with her and they mutually tranced-out. He now believed he was and could be a success, she now believed in his *potential* for success. This *mutual symbiotic relationship merger trance* left them both in pain. He, because success and money were not his thing and could not maintain merger and became distant and angry—she, because his inability to keep the merger trance going left her separate and in anxiety about separation money and survival.

Makeover Trance

A frequently heard statement is, "She'll make a better man of me," or "He'll make a better woman of me." This can relate to status, money or the illusion that the other will get you to change those parts of yourself that you do not like. But this puts too much pressure on the relationship and the other person who may unknowingly be set up to be responsible for the success or failure of this **Makeover Trance**.

The Approach-Avoidance Trance

The **Approach-Avoidance Trance** is often a signpost of an infantile, "I hate you mom for not merging with me" personality. One man I knew had an unsettled lifestyle, which involved drinking, drugs, and financial mishaps, all while he was single parenting a four-year old son. He dated a woman who was financially well-off, and conservative in her lifestyle choices. He envisioned her as the one who would tame his wild ways. Eventually he found himself baiting her and provoking arguments. Deep down, he resented the role he had put her in, and tried to bring her down to his level after he had unknowingly given up on himself ever rising to hers.

We can lie to ourselves about who our partner is, or we can delude ourselves about who we are in relationship to them. Making a long-term commitment based on illusions, self-deceptions, or fantasies and trances to avoid separation, usually sets up the relationship for eventual failure.

The Dismissing Trance

Another form of self-deception may occur in believing only what is said while dismissing evidence to the contrary displayed through actions or behavior—or the **Dismissive Trance**. One woman client believed her boyfriend when he told her he wanted a committed, long-term relationship, even though at forty-five, he had never been with one woman longer than a year. She told herself that now that he had found her, his true love, he would be different. This was a painful self-deception, which she eventually needed to confront.

The Midlife Crisis: When the Trance Didn't Work

Midlife is a time of re-evaluation, and when the pain of separation is still there, maybe it's time to change partners. The midlife period often elicits resistance to having our bodies age, and all the social implications that go with a youth-worshiping society. Having a younger, attractive partner on one's arm in a continued attempt to overcome the False Core is a familiar sight. It is obviously an attempt to hold onto youth and the admiration that such a partner may bring. In this case, the image may be more important than the actual person.

Sara, a 40 year old client, had always had the idea that being with a man of high social status would ease her separation pain. For this reason even as a young girl she saw herself as being the wife of a wealthy doctor. The status and security of this profession appealed to her as well, as feeling taken care of. She did eventually marry a doctor. Yet when he decided to leave medicine in midlife to pursue a career as a writer, Sara went through a crisis in her feelings towards her husband. Clearly she was confronted with the attachment to the image which her husband presented versus the man he was behind his professional role.

In most relationships, time creates enough personal change that if images are the key to whether one stays with another, then those images will have their opportunity to be directly confronted. With such life issues as aging bodies, career changes, parenting, and unexpected crises, images may crumble leaving what is underneath to be contended with. In other words, *images are imagined to be the cure for separation, when actually personal, professional, and relationship images are the buffer against separation, coupled with the fantasized merger.* This is why people fight so hard to keep their images. Because they believe that if they are these images, then they will merge, and if they are gone, separation and shock have to be felt.

Breaking Relationship Trances

Patterns which have been ingrained over long periods of time are not easily changed. This doesn't mean they should be ignored, but rather that they should be seen as potential red flags, and that some work needs to be done. We see this to be the case particularly in areas with a long standing history of:

—addictions
—commitment issues
—control and jealousy issues
—Impulse problems (such as rage)
—financial or career instability or irresponsibility.

The following is a series of questions that may help you uncover deceptions you may have regarding yourself or your partner.

BREAKING RELATIONSHIP TRANCES— QUESTIONNAIRE

(To be done with a partner or potential partner)

Regarding My Partner:
1. Regarding my partner, What am I unwilling to see?
   Write down or verbally say the answer until nothing more arises.

2. Regarding my partner, What do I tell myself in order to not see that?
   Write down or verbally say the answer until nothing more arises.

3. Regarding my partner, What excuses do I make for them?
   Write down or verbally say the answer until nothing more arises.

4. Regarding my partner, What an I unwilling to know?
   Write down or verbally say the answer until nothing more arises.

5. Why would I not want to know about them?
   Write down or verbally say the answer until nothing more arises.

6. How do I keep myself from knowing that?
   Write down or verbally say the answer until nothing more arises.

7. Regarding my partner, What am I unwilling to hear?
   Write down or verbally say the answer until nothing more arises.

8. Why would I not want to hear about them?
   Write down or verbally say the answer until nothing more arises.

9. How do I keep myself from hearing that?
   Write down or verbally say the answer until nothing more arises.

10. Regarding my partner, What am I unwilling to feel?
    Write down or verbally say the answer until nothing more arises.

11. Why would I not want to feel that about the relationship?
    Write down or verbally say the answer until nothing more arises.

12. How do I keep myself from feeling that?
    Write down or verbally say the answer until nothing more arises.

13. Regarding my partner, What behaviors in my partner do I knowingly or unknowingly resist?
Write down or verbally say the answer until nothing more arises.

14. Regarding my partner, What excuses do I make for their behaviors?
Write down or verbally say the answer until nothing more arises.

The Pretend Trance
15. Regarding my partner, What do I pretend matters?
Write down or verbally say the answer until nothing more arises.

16. Regarding my partner, What do I pretend doesn't matter?
Write down or verbally say the answer until nothing more arises.

17. Regarding my partner, What do I pretend they are?
Write down or verbally say the answer until nothing more arises.

18. Regarding my partner, What do I pretend they are not?
Write down or verbally say the answer until nothing more arises.

19, Regarding my partner, What do I pretend they feel?
Write down or verbally say the answer until nothing more arises.

20. Regarding my partner, What do I pretend they want?
Write down or verbally say the answer until nothing more arises.

21. Regarding my partner, What do I pretend they think?
Write down or verbally say the answer until nothing more arises.

22. Regarding my partner, What do I pretend I am?
Write down or verbally say the answer until nothing more arises.

23. Regarding my partner, What do I pretend I am not?
Write down or verbally say the answer until nothing more arises.

24. Regarding my partner, What do I pretend I feel?
Write down or verbally say the answer until nothing more arises.

25. Regarding my partner, What do I pretend I do not feel?
Write down or verbally say the answer until nothing more arises.

26. Regarding my partner, What do I pretend I believe?
Write down or verbally say the answer until nothing more arises.

27. Regarding my partner, What do I pretend I do not believe?
    Write down or verbally say the answer until nothing more arises.

28. Regarding my partner, What do I pretend I want?
    Write down or verbally say the answer until nothing more arises.

29. Regarding my partner, What do I pretend I do not want?
    Write down or verbally say the answer until nothing more arises.

30. Regarding my partner, What do I pretend I hear?
    Write down or verbally say the answer until nothing more arises.

31. Regarding my partner, What do I pretend I do not hear?
    Write down or verbally say the answer until nothing more arises.

32. Regarding my partner, What do I pretend I see?
    Write down or verbally say the answer until nothing more arises.

33. Regarding my partner, What do I pretend I do not see?
    Write down or verbally say the answer until nothing more arises.

Regarding Myself in Relationship to my Partner

34. Regarding Myself in Relationship to my Partner,
    Do I like the person I am when around them?
    Write down or verbally say the answer until nothing more arises.

35. Regarding myself in relationship to my partner,
    Is there any part of myself that I resist showing my partner? Why?
    Write down or verbally say the answer until nothing more arises.

36. Regarding myself in relationship to my partner,
    Is there anything (about myself) that I am unwilling to be?
    Write down or verbally say the answer until nothing more arises.

37. Regarding myself in relationship to my partner,
    Is there anything (about myself) that I am unwilling to know?
    Write down or verbally say the answer until nothing more arises.

38. Regarding myself in relationship to my partner,
    Is there anything about myself that I am unwilling to feel?
    Write down or verbally say the answer until nothing more arises.

39. Regarding myself in relationship to my partner,
    Is there anything (about myself) that I am unwilling to ask for?
    Write down or verbally say the answer until nothing more arises.

40. Regarding myself in relationship to my partner,
    Is there anything (about myself) that I am unwilling to have?
    Write down or verbally say the answer until nothing more arises.

41. Regarding myself in relationship to my partner,
    Is there anything (about myself) that I am unwilling to see?
    Write down or verbally say the answer until nothing more arises.

42. Regarding myself in relationship to my partner,
    Is there anything (about myself) that I am unwilling to hear?
    Write down or verbally say the answer until nothing more arises.

CONCLUSION

My teacher in India, Nisargaddata Maharaj, used to say, "In order to let go of something, you must first know what it is."

In this way, the problem is quite simple: 1) acknowledge your trances; 2) notice the separation-merger dynamic; and 3) be willing to experience what comes up.

We all concede that to have an *intimate relationship*, directness and honesty are a must—so why not now?

SIXTEEN

PROBLEMS

WHO AM I REALLY WITH?

After examining self-deceptions, which arose from the separation—expectation of merger dilemma we can get a better sense of who at a personality level our partner is and what is the truth of where we are in the relationship. We often fall in love with an image we hold in our heads rather than with who our partner truly is. An image can be about how the other appears externally. For example, we may have always wanted to be with someone very beautiful. We may have had fantasies of how this would make us appear to others—perhaps more desirable, worthwhile, powerful, valuable, adequate, lovable, etc.

THE SYMBIOTIC FALSE CORE-FALSE SELF

This can relate very strongly to our False Core-False Self, for not only does the False Self seek to overcome the False Core, it also often chooses a partner to either re-enforce or overcome the False Core. In other words by partnering with someone who has the complementary False Self to your False Core—you become one with them. The relationships which come about from this are *symbiotic* in that one's needs are so enmeshed with the other's that you can't really tell who does what to whom. This can be yet another example of what is now popularly known as co-dependency—where your "I" and their "they" are so intermixed that you feel you can gain self worth if your partner does something remarkable. It also works in reverse—if I choose someone who has a negative influence, then I can use that influence to reinforce my own feelings of worthlessness.

Louise was a client who did not trust men, and had a prior history of choosing men who would deceive her and sleep with other women. She became involved with a man who was honest, but over time, she began to lose her sexuality with him even though their intimacy continued to develop. Soon she felt no sexuality at all and put an end to the sexual aspect of the relationship. After a couple of years, her partner found a lover. When Louise discovered this, she stated, "See you can't trust men."

Terri was with Carl for many years. She came from a wealthy family, but inside she felt as though she had no value or worth. To overcome this lack of self worth, she married Carl who was a famous musician. At a superficial level all was well, but deep down it did not work because she still felt as if she had no real value and that her needs were not getting met in the relationship. Instead of seeing that she had tried to use his value and status to overcome her feelings of worthlessness, she continually tried to get him to change so that she would not feel worthless. At the same time, she also pumped him up to feel more valuable than he was so that she could feel more valuable, and less worthless, hence the symbiotic False Core-False Self.

THE FALSE CORE AND FALSE SELF
IN RELATIONSHIP: MADE SIMPLE

Everywhere we look, we can see products, activities, and media hype promoting the search for happiness, excitement, and pleasure. If we make enough money, have the perfect body, the right partner, we might not have to experience suffering. As a result, *seeking* has become a national past time. Whether it is looking for a person, an experience, a position, or enlightenment itself, the drive to seek goes on, all of it based on our deep inner experience of something inherently missing within our own being.

This feeling of something missing has been described as a gnawing emptiness, or a black hole, which then can be labeled as anything from "There's something wrong with me" to "I am worthless." People speak of feeling it in the pit of their stomachs, in their pelvis, or in their chests. It is so uncomfortable that we have devised elaborate means of avoiding it at all costs. In fact, we have built a culture rich with distractions of all kinds to hide, conceal, get rid of, not feel, mask or overcompensate for the feeling of something missing. In other words, we fill up the emptiness by overworking, overeating, drinking too much, shopping too often, watching too much TV, obsessing about our looks or your looks or having the biggest *fill in the blank*, etc. If you examine your own life, you might find your individual ways of trying to alleviate that undesirable feeling.

All of these strategies have one thing in common: They are all attempts and strategies of the False Self to overcome the unwanted feeling of the False Core. This is usually impossible since, as you know, the False Core is the one conclusion we make about ourselves, and that organizes our entire inner world. The False Self is the way we try to overcome or hide the False Core.

Again, the way that it works is like this: The False Core is felt as an intense bodily sensation since it carries a powerful nervous system response. The brain reacts by shouting out the warning, "DANGER! Do not go there! Avoid at all costs!" We then unknowingly create conclusions about the meaning of these sensation, usually with a false concept, such as, "I'm worthless, bad or alone." These conclusions are the basis and meaning of the False Core and they become the basis of our personality. We can then spend all of our lives resisting this false belief or feeling—re-creating it, re-enacting it, or re-enforcing it. In other words, it becomes the driver behind the machinery of our personality, and every time these sensations are experienced, they have the False Core belief associated with them.

THE FALSE CORE-FALSE SELF: A BRIEF REVIEW

According to Quantum Psychology, the False Core originates in the first few months of life, usually from five to fifteen months. We have seen a strong genetic proclivity, and even ancestral lineage, as to as to the False Core's manifestation. It is not unusual to find the same False Core passed from parent to child. Prior to the creation of this False Core belief, the fetus/infant resided in a state of original innocence, or **I AM-ESSENCE**. With the dawning of conscious awareness of separation from mom, there was a shock trauma to the system, and **I AM-ESSENCE** became mixed up with the pain of the trauma. From here the story unfolds as, "Danger! You are separate because there's something wrong with you, you are incomplete, you are inadequate!" etc. The nervous system is built for survival in its attempt to organize chaos. Over time, we create strategies that try to prove wrong the False Core belief. This process is called the False Self, which works to compensate for its resisted counterpart.

With all this in mind, it is easy to appreciate the power of the interaction of the False Core-False Self with our *intimate relationships*. Moreover, when the False Core-False Self is coupled with separation-resistance to separation, and confusing the levels with expectation of merger there is no wonder that *intimate relationships* both start and end on shaky ground.

SEVENTEEN

TRANSFERENCE AND COUNTER-TRANSFERENCE IN INTIMATE RELATIONSHIPS

THE RESISTANCE TO SEPARATION

The words *transference* and *counter-transference* conjure up traditional psychological processes whereby the client transfers onto the therapist (or the therapist onto the client) feelings that are associated with past relationships, usually from childhood.

In *intimate relationships*, however, we use the concept of transference to describe when a person goes into a past-time trance and unconsciously relates to their partner as if they were that small child or the parent. What causes trance-ference? The age-regressed infant, now an adult, seeks merger and fears separation by trance-ferring or projecting mom or dad on their partner. For this to occur, the adult must age-regress. In relationships, when one age-regresses, they make their partner the source of merger and separation like they did with their parents as a child. Years later, they imagine their partner as the all-knowing mom/dad and source of merger-separation.

TRANCE-FERENCE IN
ROMANTIC RELATIONSHIPS

Trance-ference in a romantic relationship can be played out in a variety of ways. One may feel as they did as a child and unknowingly view their partner as their parent. From this vantage point, a person may feel vulnerable, needy, afraid of criticism, fear abandonment, or rejected. One may look to the other to make them feel safe, get approval, or to take care of them. Though these feelings may periodically emerge in a relationship, when it is a consistent and underlying interaction, then it often is in indication of trance-ference. We all feel young and vulnerable on occasion, especially when we are exposing and entrusting our deeper selves to another. The difference is being aware of the process and remaining in present time while knowing that our partner is our equal.

I have seen many relationships with an inherent trance-ference based on the fulfillment (or lack of) of early child-like needs such as the need to be safe, the need to be taken care of, the expectation of having all needs met by a partner, the need to be the center of a partner's universe, the need for approval—just to name a few. In some relationships, when these needs are not fulfilled by the other, hostility and blame often erupt. The underlying premise arising from trance-ference is that you are there to satisfy all my needs so that I remain symbiotically fused with you in an age-regressed trance.

When we expect our partner to resolve these early issues by becoming the parent we never had, or by mind-reading and anticipating their (your partner's) behavior to be the same our parent's, then we continue to re-enact an old pattern by age-regressing, instead of having a relationship in present time. Sometimes these unresolved issues act as magnets of attraction, causing us to repeat the patterns throughout all of our romantic relationships, either by being attracted to (repetition compulsion) the same kind of partner, or dealing with the same issues over and over again. We do this unknowingly, hoping that we will *right the wrong*, or finally get what we didn't receive as a child. "Maybe this time I can get Dad to love me," or "Maybe Mom will finally think I am good enough."

WHAT CAUSES TRANCE-FERENCE?

Trance-ference is caused when someone stays stuck in the past and identifies as being a child, seeing their partner as parental or authority-type figures. Any kind of present-day separation realization, or threat to merger expectations, brings everything back. People revert to infantile yearnings, which occurred during infancy due to the shock of the Realization of Separation. When this occurs, you unconsciously make your partner into a parent and expect them to fulfill your needs and merge with you. If these issues are not identified and dismantled, they will show up in *intimate relationships*. In order to determine if there is trance-ference, when your partner is not giving you what you want, a good question to ask yourself is, "What does this bring up in me?"

Self-enquiry may reveal underlying beliefs or structures that are being acted out with one's partner. When attention is directed outwardly towards what is not right with your partner, without also examining your own reactions, you may be acting out trance-ference issues. One indicator of a child-to-parent trance-ference is a strong and continuous need for approval

TRANCE-FERENCE—QUESTIONNAIRE
(To be done with a partner or potential partner)

1. "When you need approval, how do you give up yourself?" Ask the question and write down or verbally answer until nothing pops up.

2. "What do you do to avoid criticism, abandonment, or rejection from your partner?" Ask yourself the question and write down or verbalize the answer until nothing else pops up!

3. "When you need to be taken care of how do you feel?" Ask yourself the question and write down or verbalize the answer until nothing else pops up.

4. "Do you expect your partner to know what you need and feel without your verbalizing it?" Ask yourself the question and write down or verbalize the answer until nothing else pops up.

5. "How do you expect that your partner to fill all your needs?" Ask yourself the question and write down or verbalize the answer until nothing else pops up.

6. "When you are not the center of your partner's life, what do you feel: _____?" Ask the question and write down or verbalize the answer until nothing else pops up.

7. "What are you afraid to ask for that you really want?" Ask yourself the question and write down

or verbalize the answer until nothing else pops up.

8. "To resist your partner's anger' *I*_____?" Ask yourself the question and write down or verbalize the answer until nothing else pops up.

9. "Do you stuff your own anger to _____?" Ask yourself the question and write down or verbalize the answer until nothing else pops up.

10. "To avoid conflict, opposition or confrontation, do *I*_____?" Ask yourself the question and write down or verbalize the answer until nothing else pops up.

11. "How do you react when your partner doesn't conform to your needs?" Ask yourself the question and write down or verbalize the answer until nothing else pops up.

COUNTER-TRANCE-FERENCE

Counter-trance-ference occurs when we unconsciously identify with a parent and then see our partner through that parent's eyes. We treat our partner as a child, and often keep them dependent or even helpless.

Peter and Marilyn had been married for ten years. Marilyn felt that Peter was lazy and unmotivated, and she was very angry with him. She had strong *expectations* that they both would work on their house at night after work. Peter drove 45 miles a day to a physically challenging job and when he got home at night all he wanted to do was collapse on the couch and watch TV. When Peter resisted her demands, Marilyn became intolerant and critical. Eventually their interactions became hostile.

Through therapy, Marilyn came to terms with how she was relating to Peter as her father had related to her. Her father was demanding and critical, frequently hollering at Marilyn and her siblings for being lazy. When they got home from school, the children would be forced to work around the house until bedtime. Marilyn had unconsciously taken on her father's identity and related to Peter as if he were her son. As a result, she was unable to respond to him in present time, seeing him only through her internalized father's filter.

COMMON INDICATORS OF TRANCE-FERENCE OR COUNTER-TRANCE-FERENCE:

—You continually anticipate the other's needs.
—You feel compelled to rescue your partner.
—You always feel critical or impatient with your partner.
—You do all you can to prevent discomfort for your partner.
—You analyze your partner.
—You therapize your partner.
—You diagnose your partner.
—You see your partner as a victim, helpless, or falling apart without you.

CONCLUSION

When trance-ference or counter-trance-ference occur, we are unable to experience ourselves, our partner, or the relationship in the present time. Both trance-ference and counter-trance-ference are often the cause of feelings of hidden agendas, *expectations*, power imbalances, and confusion. The uncovering and dismantling of both is fundamental to an *intimate relationship*.

EIGHTEEN

THE FALSE CORE-FALSE SELF IN RELATIONSHIP IN DEPTH

How does the False Core-False Self process pertain to relationships? Since it is the underlying motivator or driver of one's psychology, it certainly will affect one's choices, needs, assumptions, and perhaps even to whom one is attracted. As discussed earlier, it could be the underlying motive for relationship altogether. It can also be the motive as to why we choose a specific person, perhaps one who might re-enforce (enable) or help in the attempt to overcome the False Core belief.

THE MAJOR FALSE CORE-FALSE SELF

FALSE CORE DRIVERS:	FALSE SELF COMPENSATORS
1. There must be something wrong with me (I am imperfect)	I have to be perfect
2. I am worthless	I have to prove worth or value
3. I have an inability to do	I must achieve
4. I am inadequate	I must prove adequacy
5. I do not exist	I must prove existence
6. I am alone	I must connect
7. I am incomplete	I must gather experience to feel complete
8. I am powerless	I must prove I have power
9. I am loveless	I must be lovable
10. I am crazy	I must become sane or healthy
11. There is no support or safety	I must create safety or support (so I feel safe and supported)
12. I am out of control	I must control myself or others to feel in control

THE FALSE CORE-FALSE SELF AND RELATIONSHIPS

According to Freud, the nervous system organizes experiences in chains of earlier similar events, thus making the present seem like the past and creating what is commonly called a *pattern*. Simply stated, the False Core pulls your chain of associations

Laura was one client who discovered that her partners throughout her 42 years were all men she felt never really saw who she was. She never felt seen by them. In fact, she would say, "It's as if *I don't exist* around them." This pattern went back to her childhood to a very self-absorbed father who saw his children as reflections of himself. Laura was shy and sensitive as a young child who responded to her father's self-centeredness by withdrawing even more into herself. As the years went on, Laura felt *invisible* much of the time until she became involved with very intelligent, powerful men who liked engaging with her mentally. But within her relationships, the emptiness (as in a lack) was always present just as when she was a child. Laura felt that her partners never encouraged her to reveal more of herself. In this case, Laura believed the False Core idea that she did not exist, and then unconsciously chose men who reinforced her feeling of being invisible. And the pattern began with her relation to her father.

Another client, Robert, had a pattern of being with women who were emotionally or psychologically unstable. He found himself in a rescuer mode much of the time, taking on the healing of wounded women. In his own eyes, he felt better about himself when he was helping others. The unfortunate part of this dynamic was that the women he chose to relate to had so many problems, too much of his time was spent in crisis or in some drama with them. Robert began to feel drained, resentful, and unable to have his needs tended to within the relationship.

Robert realized that his False Core was a feeling of worthlessness which drove him toward problematic (crazy) women. He attempted to overcome this deep sense of having no value by becoming indispensable to someone. After dismantling this worthless identity, Robert began to lose interest in being with someone who was wounded or needy. He no longer needed the woman in his life to reflect his self-worth. Again, this was the particular False Core that he experienced as a way to deal with the shock of the Realization of Separation.

By uncovering the driving principle, the False Core belief, one will be able to have a more present-time relationship. The relationship will not need to be part of a false structure nor will one need his or her partner to participate in the upholding or defending against a concept that is false in nature and has nothing to do with who one truly is.

INTEGRATING THE BOOK

In order to integrate all we have discussed, below are included several couples sessions to demonstrate the overriding influence of the False Core-False Self in relationship:

147

COUPLES DEMONSTRATION I

Elizabeth and Fred were a couple from Canada, who participated in a Quantum Psychology training. They have volunteered to work on their relationship as a demonstration of couple's therapy techniques.

Stephen: (To Fred) What seems to be the issue for you?

Fred: My wife talks too much about therapy and spirituality and applies it to me, rather than to herself.

Stephen: What does this make you feel like?

Therapeutic Note:

It is important to focus Fred's attention on his own response to his wife rather than what she does. So often individuals hold the "other" responsible for their own internal discomfort. The real issue is what is brought up within oneself rather than getting the other to change.

Fred: I go into feeling like *there's something missing with me*, get angry, lose control, and then leave the situation.

Therapeutic Note:

From an earlier discussion, it had been noted that Fred's False Core belief that he felt *something was missing* within him. All other responses, such as the ones he mentioned here, were ways that he kept himself from feeling the empty feeling of this construct. Unless he could identify this as pulling his chain, he would continue to act out of it with his wife. Thus the

next part of the session was directed at uncovering
and dismantling the specific ways he distracted off
this issue and re-enacted it with his wife.

Stephen: What does she say that pulls this chain of reac-
            tions?

Therapeutic Note:
Attention is directed towards identifying the triggers
of Fred's reactions so that he may become aware of
what sets off the pattern.

Fred: Criticism of any kind

Stephen: Where in your body do you feel the critical
            mother? Where in your body do you feel the
            little boy who feels he is always being criticized?

Therapeutic Note:
The leap and assumption on my part is that Fred had
internalized an image of his mother criticizing him
which he unknowingly was projecting onto his wife.
Thus, the first indication of trance-ference is noted
and seen as something he had taken on.

Fred: The right side of my face, and the little boy is in
            my belly. It feels hot, angry and hypervigilant.

Stephen: Put the critical mother and the little boy who
            feels criticized over there (another part of the
            room). Notice the energy between the two.

Therapeutic Note:
By having Fred *take off* these past-time identities, he
may begin to experience himself as separate from

them, and thus be able to observe them as energy states or trances, rather than who he is *NOW* in present time.

Fred: There is a lot of aggression and tension going from the little boy who is criticized to the critical mother. The energy going from the critical mother to the criticized little boy is more controlling and she tries to give the appearance of being helpful.

Stephen: Notice where in your body you experience the False Core.

Fred: In my chest.

Stephen: Now, have a chain between the False Core of *something missing* in your chest and these reactions, with each reaction being a link of the chain. How does it feel to see this chain?

Fred: It is clear to see the connections between by False Core and the links in the chain which bring this reaction.

Stephen: Now if the False Core chain were separate from you—what would the experience be?

Fred: It really helps to see these as objects and being able to see the connection they do not seem to be this automatic thing inside of me anymore.

Stephen: Now, take the label off and have the whole chain as energy. How are you doing?

Fred: Great. Much freer.

Stephen: (To Elizabeth) What is the issue for you?

Elizabeth: Fred determines how much time allotted on
             something we do.

Stephen: Who modeled this for you? And what would
             come up for you when this would happen?

Elizabeth: My mother. I would feel shame and like I would
             have to fight for my space, but *I feel alone.*

Stephen: Notice where in your body is the mother *deter-
             miner* and where in your body is the ashamed
             little girl who fights for space. Place them over
             there (another part of the room) and notice how
             they are connected.

Therapeutic Note:

Once again, there is the need to identify the source,
i.e., mom, in this case, and externalize these reactions
or identities in order to gain some present-time space.

Stephen: (To the couple) Now turn and face each other.
             Elizabeth, place an image of your mother next
             to Fred. Fred, place an image of your mother
             next to Elizabeth. Now, Elizabeth, say to each
             member of the group: "This is my husband,
             and this is my mother. They are similar because
             and *(fill in the blank)*. Then say, "They are dif-
             ferent because. . . ."

(Repeat process for Fred)

Therapeutic Note:

Each partner now begins to see how they have un-knowingly been relating to the other through the lens of a past-time relationship to a parent. After identify-ing the ways they project this image onto the other, they are asked to *bust* the trance-ference in present time by stating how their partner is different from their parent.

Stephen: Now look and see the chain of associations and reactions and how they are connected to each of your False Cores. Fred, yours being the False Core that *something is missing*; and Elizabeth, yours being the False Core of *being alone* which you identified earlier in the session.

Therapeutic Note:

At this point Fred realized that he had taken on his father's pain in relationship to his mother and fused with his father.

Stephen: Fred, place the father identity over there (in an-other space in the room), and then make this statement: "My father is still holding on. And I thought I was my father."

Fred: "My father is still holding on. And I thought I was my father."

Stephen: Now say, "I took on my father's feelings to help him." Notice where in your body are your father's feelings. De-label them and give them back to your father.

Therapeutic Note:

This was a very powerful part of the session for Fred. His father had attempted to hang himself, and though he survived, it had caused enough physical damage to leave him disabled and depressed the rest of his life. Fred needed to see how he had taken on his father's suffering as well, as the False Core belief from his father that *something was missing*. He even noted that he was continuing to carry in his own body some of the rope that his father had tried to kill himself with. Fred became very tearful yet emotionally freed as a result of this piece of work.

Stephen: Now say to Elizabeth, "I was holding onto my father's pain with my mother. I thought I had to feel it for him.? Now say, "I thought I was re-sisting *my* feelings, but I was really resisting my father's feelings."

Therapeutic Note:

At this point the painful feelings and the sense of hav-ing the rope around him were given back to Fred's father as energy. Fred was able to be in a more open place where he could observe his own False Core chain of reactions and his true nature prior to the taking on of this chain.

Stephen: Make eye contact with each other and experi-ence the **ESSENCE**-to-**ESSENCE** resonance between you both. Notice at another level there is only one substance, not two. Notice the **BIG EMPTINESS** that joins you both. How are you both now?

Fred: Great.

Elizabeth: Much freer, much more space.

IMAGES

Images may pertain to behaviors, style, intellectual personas the other exhibits. But mostly they are derived from ideas or models internalized from our environment. They can be mom or dad's image of who they wanted us to be with, or a societal image that the culture has infused us with through the media. We have unknowingly bought into external images of what makes a good partner, whether from the television show *Father knows Best*, or from *James Bond* movies. We have internalized the myths about love and romance and continue to seek out a fairytale ending.

Sometimes the image will be around an ideal I have about relationship. We may carry an image about a conflict-free relationship and then choose a passive or co-dependent partner in order to maintain the image that we never fight. Usually, an image will relate directly back to you and how you wither want or don't want to see yourself or to be seen by others.

QUESTIONS TO ASK ONESELF

**(Answers are to be written down or
said verbally to/with a partner or potential partner)**

Regarding relationships:

1.   Regarding relationships, Do I seek out being with a powerful person in order to feel or appear more powerful or less powerless?

2. Regarding relationships, Do I seek out being with a perfect person in order to feel or appear more perfect or less imperfect?

3. Regarding relationships, Do I seek out being with a loving person in order to feel or appear more loving or less loveless?

4. Regarding relationships, Do I seek out being with a adequate person in order to feel or appear more adequate or less inadiquate?

5. Regarding relationships, Do I seek out being with a knowledgeable person in order to feel or appear more knowledgeable or less ignorant?

6. Regarding relationships, Do I seek out being with an achieving person in order to feel or appear more achieving or less impotent?

7. Regarding relationships, Do I seek out being with a worthy person in order to feel or appear more worthy or less worthless?

8. Regarding relationships, Do I seek out being with a connected person in order to feel or appear more connected or less alone?

9. Regarding relationships, Do I seek out being with a person who has status in order to feel or appear as though I am more conplete?

10. Regarding relationships, How do I want to appear to others?

11. Regarding relationships, How do I want my partner to appear to others?

12. Regarding relationships, I do not want my partner to be seen as _____.

13. Regarding relationships, Mom's image of the perfect partner for me was _____.

14. Regarding relationships, Dad's image of the perfect partner for me was _____.

15. Regarding relationships, In my family it was not acceptable to be _____.

16. Regarding relationships, In my family it was important to be _____.

17. Regarding relationships, I want a perfect person to _____.

18. Regarding relationships, I want a valuable person to _____.

19. Regarding relationships, I want an achieving person to _____.

20. Regarding relationships, I want a powerful person to _____.

21. Regarding relationships, I want a connected person to _____.

22. Regarding relationships, I want a person with status to _____.

23. Regarding relationships, I want a person with lots of experience to _____.

24. Regarding relationships, I want a loving person to _____.

25. Regarding relationships, I want a sane person to _____.

Review your answers to see if they reflect on your choice in a partner. How attached are you to having this image or its opposite (reaction to) in your partner or relationship? Would you stay with this person if this image changed? How would your feelings towards them change, if at all?

COUPLES DEMONSTRATION II

George and Paula are a couple from Maine who participated in a Quantum Psychology training and volunteered to work on their relationship in a demonstration of couple's therapy techniques. During the training, George had been working on the False Core issue of *I am worthless*. Paula's issue was *I am inadequate*. This session was specifically directed at how George and Paula would unconsciously relate to each other through the lens of their False Cores and the dismantling of the automatic tendency to do so.

Stephen: (To George) Who modeled *worthless* for you?

George: My mother.

Stephen: And who modeled *trying to prove worth*?

George: My father

Stephen: (To Paula) Who modeled trying to *prove you were not inadequate*?

Paula: My mother.

Stephen: How does this manifest in your relationship?

George: I recognize that I fuse my mother with Paula.

Paula: I fuse George with my Dad. My parents got divorced when I was small. I feel deserted by my dad. I was his favorite. We were one, and then he wasn't there anymore. Now, it is very clear that I look to George to give me what I missed from dad.

Stephen: For you, George becomes like your dad. Can you tell me one problem which arises from this in your relationship?

George: I always have the feeling like I am more like a father to Paula than like a husband. When I was a kid, my father was away a lot and I had the feeling like I had to replace my father and take care of my mother.

Therapeutic Note:

Here is a good example of how trance-ference and counter-trance-ference are acted out within a relationship. Neither partner is relating to the other in present time.

Stephen: So, you became a father replacement and you are trying to *prove worth* like your father. So George tries to prove worth. And Paula?

Paula: I take on the little girl trying to seek attention.

Stephen: George, find where in your body is the *worthless little boy identity,* and *where in your body is the "I have to prove worth" identity.* Take them off and place them on the other side of the room. Now, Paula, you do the same with the *inadequate little girl and the "I have to prove adequacy" identity.* George, very slowly, take on the worthless identity and look through it like a lens or a pair of glasses. How does Paula seem to you through that lens?

George: Somebody who can help me prove worth. It feels like a distance has come between us. I feel like I am tossed into this reaction and I can blame her for doing this.

Stephen: (To Paula) When George took on this lens, is there a tendency for you to take on the *I have to prove adequacy lens*?

Paula: Absolutely. And it feels like I am creating *expectations.* I feel anxious and like there is pressure.

Stephen: Now each of you take off the lens and feel the warmth, the love of the **ESSENCE-to-ES-SENCE** resonance.

Therapeutic Note:
By having each partner intentionally put their lenses (False Core-False Self) on and off several times and view each other through them, they were able to ob-

serve the effect of relating to each other through their False Cores'.

Stephen:	George, take on the *worthless lens*, look at Paula and say, "You're, Paula, you are *not* my mother, my father, my teacher, sister, etc."
George:	You're Paula, you are not my mother, my father, my teacher, sister, etc.
Stephen:	Now, imagine all those people are all around her. If she is not all of these images, what is your experience like looking at her right now?
George:	More close.
Stephen:	*Put on the worthless lens*, look through it and tell me a similarity between Paula and all of these people (images).
George:	*I am worthless* and she is not. These identities look down on me, like Paula does (when I am in the worthless False Core).
Stephen:	Now take off the *worthless lens* and tell me a difference between Paula and all these people.
George:	Paula is someone I feel close to. I feel close to others in a different way. I feel comfortable with Paula, I don't with those others. Paula is my lover, the others are not.

Therapeutic Note:

The *associational trance* occurs when one loses present time and then the partner becomes like a parent or perhaps several "past significant people", as was the case with George. That tendency only comes with the False Core lens (glasses). When one is in **ESSENCE**, there are no associations, no lens. The strong urge to put the lens back on must be lessened.

Stephen: Paula, pick up the little girl identity (lens) and notice how George looks to you through that lens. Notice the similarities between George and your dad.

Paula: He looks scary.

Stephen: Take the lens off and tell me some difference between George and your dad?

Paula: He's a whole different person.

Stephen: George, put the *I have to prove worth* lens on and looking at Paula, I want you to say, "You are Paula, you are not my mother, my daughter, my sister, my brother, etc."

George: You are Paula, you are not my mother, my daughter, my sister, my brother, etc.

Stephen: With the lens on, notice all these people around her. Intentionally, create the distance you feel when you have the lens on, and notice how Paula appears to look as you do that. Create it several times.

George: She looks distant and angry.

Stephen: Now uncreate it. Notice when it is there, there is a separation. See all these people as separate from Paula. Do that a couple of times.

George: I feel like she moves away, and then with the people out of her or *not her*, she comes closer.

Stephen: Where in your body to you feel that Essential Love?

George: My heart.

Stephen: Allow it to spread throughout your body. (To Paula) Pick up the *I have to prove adequacy* lens and look through it and say, "You are George, you are not my mother, my daughter, my sister, my brother, etc."

Paula: You are George, you are not my dad, my mom, my brother.

Stephen: Take the lens on and have all the people merge with George, then take the lens off and have the people separate from George. Do this a few times.

Therapeutic Note:

Being able to recognize the result of relating to one's partner through the lens of an identity or one's past, is the first step. Then, we want to separate the partner from all of the people projected onto them. Over and over, we present the opportunity to view the other with and without the lens, noticing the difference in how love, and relationship in present time is lost when we stay in the past-time False Core-False Self.

Stephen: (to Paula) Notice where in your body you feel the Essential Love.

Paula: My stomach.

Stephen: Allow it to spread throughout your body. How are you both doing?

Paula: It was an incredible experience. When I put the lens on, it was like George was two different people.

George: It feels like a new feeling of love, more intense than ever before.

CONCLUSION

Until trance-ference and counter-trance-ference is broken it is impossible to have an *intimate relationship*. Why? Because, we are not in present time, rather, we are in past time expecting and wishing others to merge with us and take away our past-time pain.

MERGER AND SEPARATION ARE LIKE THE
TIDES OF THE OCEAN—THEY CONTINUALLY
ARISE AND SUBSIDE. ANY ATTEMPT *TO
RESIST SEPARATION OR MAKE MERGER
HAPPEN* IS LIKE TRYING TO
CONTROL THE OCEAN.

Stephen H. Wolinsky

REFERENCES

Agneesens, C. (Forthcoming*). The Fabric of Wholeness: Biological Intelligence and Relational Gravity.*

American College Dictionary. (1963). New York: Random House.

Arica Institute, Inc., The. (1989). The Arican. New York.

Blanck, G., & Rubin. *Ego psychology II.* New York: Columbia Univ. Press.

Blanck, G., & Rubin. (1979). *Ego psychology II: Psychoanalytic developmental psychology.* New York: Columbia University Press.

Bollas, C. (1987). *The shadow of the object: Psychoanalysis of the unthought known.* New York: Columbia Univ. Press

Bollas, C. (1989). *Furies of destine: Psychoanalysis and human idiom.* London: Free Association Volumes

Bourland, D., & Johnson, P. (1991). *To Be or Not: An e-prime anthology.* San Francisco: International Society for General Semantics.

Horner, A. J. (1985). *Object relations and the developing ego in therapy*. Northridge, NJ: Jason Arunsun, Inc.

Johnson, Stephen (1987). *Humanizing the narcissistic style*. NY/London: W.W. Norton & Co.

Johnson, S. M. (1987). *Humanizing the narcissistic style*. New York: The Arica Institute, Inc.

Johnson, S. M. (1991). *The symbiotic character*. NY/London: W. W. Norton & Co.

Korzybski, A. (1993). *Science and sanity*. Englewood, NJ: Institute for General Semantics.

Korzybski, A. (1962). *Selections from science and sanity*. Englewood, NJ: International Non-Aristotelian Library Publishing Company.

Irving J. L. (1941). *Language habits in human affairs*. England, New Jersey: International Society for General Semantics

Mahler, M. (1968). *On the human symbiosis and vicissitudes of individuation*. New York: International Universe Press.

Marshall, R. J., & Marshall, S. V. (1988). *The transference-counter-transference matrix: The emotional-cognitive dialogue in psychotherapy, psychoanalysis and supervision*. New York: Columbia University Press.

Mckay, M., D., M., & Fanning, P. (1981). *Thoughts and feelings: The art of cognitive stress intervention*. Oakland, CA: Harbinger Publications.

Naranjo, E. (1990). *Enneatype structures: Self analysis for the seeker*. CA: Gateways IDHHB, Inc.

Nicoll, M. (1984). *Psychological commentaries on the teaching of Gurdjieff and Ouspensky*. Vol. 1. Boulder/London: Shambhala.

Nisargadatta, Majaraj. *I am That*. 1994. Durham, NC: Acorn Press

Ouspensky, P. D. *In search of the miraculous*. 1949. New York: Harcourt, Brace and World, Inc.

Palmer, H. (1988). *The enneagram*. CA: Harper & Row.

Reich, W. (1942). *The function of the orgasm*. The discovery of the orgone. New York: World Publishing.

Singh, J. (1979). *Vijnanabhairava or divine consciousness*. Delhi: Motilal Banarsidass.

Suzuki, S. *Zen mind, beginner's mind*. New York: Weatherhill, 1970.

Weinberg, H. L. (1959). *Levels of knowing and existence: Studies in general semantics*. Englewood, NJ: Institute of General Semantics.

Wolinsky, S. H. (1993). *The dark side of the inner child*. Norfolk, CT: Bramble Co.

Wolinsky, S. H. (1991). *Trances people live: Healing approaches to quantum psychology*. Norfolk, CT: Bramble Co.

Wolinsky, S. H. (1993). *Quantum consciousness*. Norfolk, CT: Bramble Books.

Wolinsky, S. H. (1995). *Hearts on Fire*. Norfolk, CT: Bramble Books.

Wolinsky, S. H. (1994). *The tao of chaos: Quantum consciousness*. Vol. II. Norfolk, CT: Bramble Books.

Wolinsky, S. H. (1999). *The way of the human*. Vol. 1: *Developing multi-dimensional awareness*. CA: Quantum Research Institute Press.

Wolinsky, S. H. (1999). *The way of the human*. Vol. II: *The False Core-False Self*. CA: Quantum Research Institute Press.

Wolinsky, S. H. (1999). *The way of the human*. Vol. III: *Beyond Quantum Psychology*. CA: Quantum Research Institute Press.

Wolinsky, S. H. (2000). *I AM THAT I AM: A tribute to Sri Nisargadatta Maharaj*. CA: Quantum Research Institute Press.

Wolinsky, S. H. (2000). *Intimate relationship: Why they do and do not work*. CA: Quantum Research Institute Press.